IN THE KITCHEN

with

Bonnie Stern

COOKBOOK

& VIDEO Canada am

INFACT PUBLISHING LTD./CTV TELEVISION NETWORK

INFACT Publishing Ltd.
66 Portland St.
2nd Floor
Toronto, ON
M5V 2M8

ISBN: 1-896092-01-2

Cover design: Donna Guilfoyle/ArtPlus Ltd.
Text design: Sylvia Vander Schee/ArtPlus Ltd.
Video digitization: Brant Cowie/ArtPlus Ltd.

Printed in Canada by Metropole Litho

Contents

Introduction

For me, a cooking teacher and cookbook author, this project is a dream come true—a chance to write a cookbook and demonstrate the techniques involved in the recipes. The goal behind all my cooking classes during the past twenty-three years has been to make cooking easier, more fun and more successful for students. But, ultimately, my school is very small, so this video and book now gives me the opportunity to bring my school to many more people.

Watch the video and then find the recipe in the book. When you make the recipe yourself, check back to the video if there is something you don't understand. There are many more recipes in the book than on the video, but most use similar techniques. I hope you'll try some of them. Because I have a strong interest in healthful cooking, the book also includes low-fat tips wherever possible (in some cases, low-fat alternatives are not practical so it may be better just to eat a small portion—moderation is always a good policy!)

A project like this is more involved than even I could have imagined. It was a great learning experience for everyone, especially me, and there are many people to thank.

Once again, I was dazzled by the professionalism, talent and energy of my staff. Very special thanks go to Anne Apps, Lorraine Butler, Rhonda Caplan, Letty Lastima, Julie Lewis, Maureen Lollar, Melissa Mertl and Linda Stephen.

Thanks also to my family: Mark, Anna, Fara and Ray Rupert; Jane, Meredith, Charles and Wayne Krangle; and Max and Ruth Stern.

Finally, thanks to John Cassaday, Jay Cohen, Sidney Cohen, Fiona Conway, Brant Cowie, Cathy Cripps, Glen Dickout, Donna Guilfoyle, Randy Gulliver, Marian Hebb, Brian Hunt, Laura, Victor Levin, Bonnie Mactavish, Phil Pendry, Alex Pero, Frank Prest, Rose Snukal, Judi Ritter, Rob Roy, Shelley Tanaka, Sylvia Vander Schee, Kai Voigt, Cindy Winstone and, especially, Susan Yates.

Bonnie Stern

1 Spreads and Dips

TECHNIQUES AND TIPS

- Spreads and dips are easy to make, and you can whip one up at the last minute. Hummos, for example (page 10), uses ingredients that you can keep on hand at all times.
- Dips and spreads make great sandwich spreads, salad dressings, fillings for hollowed-out vegetables (e.g., tomatoes or mushrooms), toppings for baked potatoes, garnishes for soups, or sauces for roasted meat or fish; some are even great on pasta.
- To make a dip more spreadable (to use in sandwiches, for example), use less mayonnaise, sour cream, yogurt or other liquid in the mixture; or add cream cheese, ricotta cheese, chèvre (goat cheese) or yogurt cheese (page 14). To turn a spread into a dip or salad dressing, add more mayonnaise, sour cream, milk or yogurt to the mixture.
- Serve dips and spreads with crackers, breadsticks, corn chips, bread, toast, pita chips or bagel chips (page 16), grilled bread (page 15), or with an array of vegetables. Certain vegetables (carrots, beans, broccoli, snow peas and asparagus, for example) will become brighter and fresher looking if they are partially boiled (blanched) before being used for dipping. Simply plunge them into boiling water for about 2 minutes (snow peas need only 30 seconds). Immerse them in ice water to stop the cooking and keep the texture firm, and then pat dry.

- *If you want your spreads or dips to be very smooth, use a food processor or blender to blend ingredients. But if you want the mixture to be slightly chunky, have ingredients such as cheese or butter at room temperature, chop vegetables finely and combine with a whisk or spoon. Sometimes you may want to combine both methods. If there are a lot of fresh herbs in a recipe but you do not want the dip to turn "green," process all ingredients except the herbs in the machine, then stir in the chopped herbs by hand at the end.*
- *Many people express concern about "double-dipping" vegetables (taking a bite and dipping again), but if you cut the vegetables into bite-sized pieces, this shouldn't be a problem.*
- *To lower the fat content in dips and spreads, use yogurt, yogurt cheese (page 14), low-fat mayonnaise, sour cream, cream cheese and lower-fat hard cheeses instead of the higher-fat versions.*

TECHNIQUE REVIEW

See this on the video

The Haas avocado, on the left, is the best for guacamole.

After rotating the two halves of the avocado, it will open nicely.

Dice the avocado in its skin by cutting through the flesh.

Then, scoop it out into a salsa-type mixture.

After mashing the avocado and salsa, taste with a corn chip to test for the correct amount of salt.

Guacamole (facing page) excellent on its own, can also be used as a sauce for grilled steak.

Guacamole

See this on the video

The larger, smooth-skinned light-green avocados may be beautiful, but the ugly, dark Haas ones are more "buttery" and less watery. Watch the video to see how to remove the pit and dice the avocado easily. Unripe avocados have virtually no flavour, but it can be hard to find ripe ones the day you need them, so buy them a few days ahead of time. Let unripe avocados ripen on the counter (placing them in a paper bag will speed the ripening process); if they are already ripe, refrigerate.

Serve this dip with tortilla chips or pita chips (page 16) or use as a sandwich filling, as a topping for chili or fajitas (page 30), or as a sauce with grilled steak or lamb.

Makes about 2 cups/500 mL

1	small tomato, seeded (page 00) and diced	1
1	clove garlic, minced	1
1/4 cup	finely chopped red onion	50 mL
1	jalapeño chile, finely chopped	1
3 tbsp	lime juice	45 mL
1/2 tsp	salt	2 mL
1/3 cup	finely chopped fresh cilantro or parsley	75 mL
2	ripe avocados	2

1. Combine tomato, garlic, onion, chile, lime juice, salt and cilantro.

2. Cut avocado in half and gently rotate halves to separate. Remove pit by piercing with a knife and jiggling gently to loosen. Holding the avocado half in the palm of your hand, gently dice avocado through to the skin and then scoop into tomato mixture with a larger spoon. With a potato masher or fork, mash gently so that some of the avocado is still chunky, but the rest is pureed to hold the mixture together. Taste and adjust seasonings if necessary. Serve immediately if possible, or cover with plastic wrap directly on surface of dip to prevent discoloration.

Hint:

To get the most juice from a lime, pierce it in a few places, put in a glass measure and microwave on High for 30 seconds. Cool. Cut in half and juice.

A Lighter Side:

Use cooked asparagus, cooked green peas, yogurt cheese (page 14) or low-fat ricotta cheese in place of half the avocado.

Hummos with Tahini

The tahini (sesame seed paste) for this popular Middle Eastern chickpea spread is available at health food stores. Serve hummos as a dip with pita chips (page 16), use it to fill mini pitas (page 12), or use it as a sandwich spread.

Makes about 2 cups/500 mL

1	19-oz/540-mL tin chickpeas, rinsed and drained	1
2	cloves garlic, minced	2
3 tbsp	lemon juice	45 mL
3 tbsp	olive oil	45 mL
1/4 tsp	hot red pepper sauce (or to taste)	1 mL
1/2 tsp	ground cumin	2 mL
1/2 tsp	salt	2 mL
1/4 tsp	pepper	1 mL
1/2 cup	tahini paste	125 mL
Garnish:	Lemon slices	
	Sprigs of cilantro or parsley	

1. Place chickpeas in food processor fitted with steel blade. Blend coarsely.

2. Add garlic, lemon juice, olive oil, hot pepper sauce, cumin, salt and pepper. Blend in tahini. Puree until as smooth as you wish. Taste and adjust seasonings if necessary.

3. Spread hummos in shallow serving bowl and surround with lemon slices and sprigs of cilantro.

A Lighter Side:

Use yogurt or yogurt cheese (page 14) instead of olive oil; use 2 tsp/10 mL dark sesame oil instead of tahini paste.

Fresh Tomato Salsa

This tomato salsa has the fresh, lively taste and texture I think salsas should have. It's fast, easy and versatile. Serve it on top of grilled bread (page 15), as a garnish for soups, or as a sauce with grilled fish or chicken.

Makes about 1-1/2 cups/375 mL

2 tbsp	olive oil	25 mL
1 tbsp	red wine vinegar or lime juice	15 mL
1	clove garlic, minced	1
1 tsp	salt	5 mL
1/4 tsp	pepper	1 mL
1	small jalapeño chile, finely chopped	1
2	tomatoes, seeded and diced	2
1/2 cup	finely chopped fresh basil or cilantro	125 mL

1. Whisk together oil, vinegar, garlic, salt and pepper.
2. Add chile, tomatoes and basil. Taste and adjust seasonings if necessary.

Hint:
Many people with sensitive skin like to wear plastic gloves when handling hot chiles.

Hint:
Remove seeds and ribs from jalapeños for a milder taste.

Hint:
To remove seeds, cut tomatoes in half crosswise and gently squeeze out seeds.

A Lighter Side:
Omit the olive oil.

Crab Dip with Mini Pitas

Many dips can be served in tiny pita pockets. Cut mini pitas in half; the pockets make perfect cups. This dip can also be made with finely chopped smoked salmon, or even well-drained canned crab, salmon or tuna. To turn this into a spread, use less mayonnaise and sour cream.

Makes about 1-1/4 cups/300 mL

4 oz	cream cheese with herbs and garlic (e.g., Boursin or Rondele)	125 g
1/3 cup	mayonnaise	75 mL
1/3 cup	sour cream or unflavoured yogurt	75 mL
3-1/2 oz	frozen crabmeat, defrosted, picked over, squeezed dry and shredded	100 g
1/4 tsp	pepper	1 mL
1 tbsp	lemon juice	15 mL
10	mini pitas, cut in half	10

A Lighter Side:
Use low-fat cream cheese and mayonnaise; be sure to use low-fat yogurt in place of the sour cream.

1. Beat cheese until creamy. Stir in mayonnaise and sour cream.

2. Stir in crab. Add pepper and lemon juice. Taste and adjust seasonings if necessary (cheese and crab are usually quite salty).

3. Stuff pita halves with dip.

Herbed Chèvre Dip

Although many people don't like chèvre (goat cheese) eaten straight, they will often love it when it is used in a recipe like this, because the flavour is much milder. Look for an unripened mild goat cheese with a creamy consistency. There are a few good domestic brands of chèvre, so it is usually easy to find, but if it is not available in your supermarket, look in specialty cheese shops.

Serve this with an array of raw and blanched vegetables (page 6), as a salad dressing or pasta sauce, or on potato salads.

Makes about 1 cup/250 mL

A Lighter Side:

Be sure to use low-fat yogurt instead of sour cream.

8 oz	chèvre (goat cheese)	250 g
1/2 cup	sour cream or unflavoured yogurt	125 mL
2	small cloves garlic, minced	2
1/4 tsp	hot red pepper sauce	1 mL
1 tbsp	fincly chopped fresh rosemary, or 1/2 tsp/2 mL dried	15 mL
1 tbsp	finely chopped fresh thyme, or 1/2 tsp/2 mL dried	15 mL
2 tbsp	finely chopped fresh basil or parsley	25 mL
1/2 tsp	pepper	2 mL
1/4 cup	milk	50 mL

1. Blend chèvre with sour cream until smooth.

2. Blend in garlic, hot pepper sauce, rosemary, thyme, basil and pepper.

3. Add enough milk to turn mixture into a dip. Taste and adjust seasonings if necessary.

Yogurt Cheese

Yogurt cheese is becoming so popular that it is now available commercially in some areas, but if it isn't, just make your own. There are also yogurt cheese makers on the market now.
Use yogurt cheese in place of sour cream for a lower-fat dip or topping for baked potatoes, or in place of sour cream, cream cheese or mayonnaise in spreads, salad dressings and sandwich fillings. It also makes a wonderful garnish in soups, or you can mix it with sugar, honey or maple syrup for a dessert topping.

Makes about 1-1/2 cups/ 375 mL

3 cups	**unflavoured natural yogurt**	**750 mL**
	(regular or low-fat)	

1. Line a strainer with cheesecloth, paper towel or coffee filter. Place over bowl.

2. Place yogurt in strainer. Cover with plastic wrap. Allow to rest from 3 hours to overnight. Approximately half the volume of yogurt will strain out into the bowl. The longer it sits, the thicker the yogurt cheese becomes.

3. Discard liquid (or use for cooking rice or making bread) and spoon thickened yogurt cheese into another container. Cover and use as required.

YOGURT CHEESE DIP:

Combine 1-1/2 cups/375 mL yogurt cheese with 2 minced cloves garlic and 3 tbsp/45 mL each finely chopped fresh cilantro, parsley and chives. Add 1 tbsp/15 mL finely chopped fresh tarragon (or a pinch dried), 1/2 tsp/ 2 mL salt and 1/4 tsp/1 mL each pepper and hot red pepper sauce. Serve with vegetables for dipping.

Makes about 1-1/2 cups/375 mL

Grilled Bread with Rosemary and Garlic

This makes a great appetizer on its own, but it is also great as a base for salsa (page 11) and spreads.

If you are using a skinny French baguette instead of a normal-sized loaf, you should have enough oil mixture for at least 16 small rounds.

Makes 8 slices

A Lighter Side:
Use half the olive oil.

1/3 cup	olive oil	75 mL
2	cloves garlic, minced	2
1 tbsp	finely chopped fresh rosemary, or 1/2 tsp/2 mL dried	15 mL
1/2 tsp	salt (or to taste)	2 mL
1/2 tsp	pepper	2 mL
8	slices French or Italian bread, about 3/4 inch/2 cm thick	8

1. Combine olive oil with garlic, rosemary, salt and pepper.

2. With a pastry brush, brush oil mixture over one side of bread.

3. Preheat barbecue or broiler. Grill oiled side of bread until lightly browned. Turn bread and cook second side. On barbecue, grill for about 1 minute per side. Under broiler, grill for about 2 minutes per side. Serve hot or at room temperature.

Bagel Chips/Pita Chips

This is a terrific way to use up leftover bagels or pita breads. Use the chips as snacks with dips or as croutons in salads.

Makes about 3 dozen bagel chips and 4 dozen pita chips

3	bagels	3
3 tbsp	butter, melted	45 mL
2 tbsp	sesame seeds	25 mL
3	8-inch/20 cm pita breads	3
1/4 cup	olive oil	50 mL
1 tsp	dried oregano	5 mL

1. Cut bagels in half vertically (you'll end up with two C-shaped pieces). Stand halves up on the cut side. With a sharp serrated knife, slice bagels into the thinnest slices possible. Arrange slices on baking sheet in single layer.

2. Brush slices with melted butter and sprinkle with sesame seeds. Bake in preheated 350°F/180°C oven for 10 to 15 minutes, or until crisp.

3. Separate each pita into two flat circles. Brush bumpy sides with olive oil and sprinkle with oregano. Cut each circle into 2-inch/5 cm triangles. Arrange in single layer on baking sheet. Bake in a preheated 350°F/180°C oven for 12 to 15 minutes, or until dry and crisp. Cool.

4. Store chips in an airtight container or freeze.

A Lighter Side:

Use half the amount of butter and oil, or omit butter and oil entirely and brush bagels and breads with lightly beaten egg white.

Feta Cheese Spread

Use this spread on sandwiches, or serve it with bagels or bagel chips (facing page). You can also serve it in small ramekins, as a table spread (in place of butter or margarine), or turn it into a great dip or pasta sauce by adding yogurt or cream.

Makes about 2 cups/500 mL

A Lighter Side:
Use low-fat ricotta or yogurt cheese (page 14) instead of the ricotta.

1	clove garlic, minced	1
2	anchovies, minced or	2
	1 tsp/5 mL anchovy paste	
8 oz	ricotta cheese	250 g
8 oz	feta cheese	250 g
2	green onions, finely chopped	2
1/2 tsp	dried thyme, or	2 mL
	2 tbsp/25 mL fresh	
1/2 tsp	dried oregano, or	2 mL
	1 tbsp/15 mL fresh	
1/4 tsp	hot red pepper sauce	1 mL
1/2 tsp	pepper	2 mL

1. In food processor or blender, combine garlic, anchovies, ricotta and feta. Blend until smooth.

2. Blend in green onions, thyme, oregano, hot pepper sauce and pepper. Taste and adjust seasonings if necessary.

2 Salads

TECHNIQUES AND TIPS

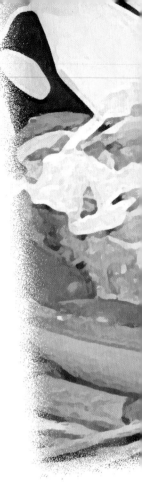

- *Wash salad greens well before using.*
- *Often it is a smart idea to have your greens in bite-sized pieces so that guests do not need knives. This is especially true for buffets, where people may be eating from plates resting on their laps.*
- *Salad greens should be well dried before being tossed with the dressing. The dressing will slide off wet greens, and water will dilute the dressing.*
- *Salad greens and herbs keep well when they are washed, dried and wrapped in tea towels or paper towels and then placed in an airtight container in the refrigerator.*
- *For easy tossing, place the dressing in the bottom of the bowl and then place the greens on top. Use a large bowl for tossing salads.*
- *Tongs work well for tossing and serving salads.*
- *Add variety to your salads by changing the greens, vinegars, oils, herbs and mustards that you use.*
- *Try adding different garnishes such as crumbled cheese, toasted nuts, homemade croutons or edible flowers.*
- *If you use sweet-tasting vinegars like balsamic, raspberry, sherry, rice or good-quality red wine vinegar, you can reduce the amount of oil in the dressing.*
- *For a lower-fat salad dressing, replace some of the oil with fruit juice, vegetable juice, fruit or vegetable puree, chicken stock, unflavoured yogurt, yogurt cheese (page 14) or buttermilk.*
- *Extra-virgin olive oil is great to use in salad dressings. Although it is more expensive than regular olive oil, it has a fruitier taste and less acidity, so you do not need to use as much (and you are at least adding great flavour along with the calories!).*

- *A dash of sesame oil makes a dressing taste very exotic. The dark, roasted, Asian variety is very potent. It is generally used in small amounts as a seasoning rather than a cooking oil. Nut oils (such as walnut and hazelnut) also add flavour to dressings.*
- *All oils go rancid eventually, so it is better to buy them in small quantities. Nut oils and sesame oil should be refrigerated after opening. Olive oils should be stored in a cool, dark place and used within a few months.*
- *Salad dressings made with olive oil should be served at room temperature, as the oil thickens when refrigerated.*
- *To test your dressing before tossing it with the salad, taste it on some of the ingredients rather than on a spoon or your finger.*
- *Many salad dressings can be used as dips and sandwich spreads.*
- *Leftover homemade bread and interesting bakery breads can be used to make delicious homemade croutons. Cut the bread into cubes, toss with olive oil, herbs and/or cheese if desired. Spread in a single layer on a baking sheet and bake at 350°F/180°C for 20 to 30 minutes, or until crisp. Use immediately or freeze.*

TECHNIQUE REVIEW

See this on the video

Romaine lettuce is the basis for a Caesar salad.

You can break the leaves into bite-sized pieces or leave them whole.

Whisk the dressing ingredients together.

Be patient when you toss the lettuce and dressing to avoid using too much dressing.

Caesar Salad (facing page) made with slivers of Parmesan cheese.

Caesar salad dressing also makes a wonderful vegetable dip.

Caesar Salad

See this on the video

There are many different versions of Caesar salad. Some add shrimp or grilled chicken. Some have huge homemade croutons, and some leave the lettuce in whole pieces. In the video, my version has slices of Parmesan cheese and lettuce in bite-sized pieces.

This versatile dressing can be used on pasta salads, as a dip for vegetables or chicken wings (page 58), or even as a topping on baked potatoes.

Use the best-quality Parmesan cheese you can find (preferably Parmigiano Reggiano).

Makes about 6 servings

1/4 cup	mayonnaise	50 mL
2 tbsp	red wine vinegar	25 mL
2	anchovies, mashed, or 1 tsp/5 mL anchovy paste	2
2	cloves garlic, minced	2
1 tsp	Dijon mustard	5 mL
1/4 tsp	pepper	1 mL
1/4 cup	olive oil	50 mL
1/2 cup	grated Parmesan cheese (preferably Parmigiano Reggiano)	125 mL
1	large head Romaine lettuce, washed, dried and broken into bite-sized pieces (about 8 cups/2 L)	1
6	slices bacon, cooked until crisp and diced, optional	6
1-1/2 cups croutons (page 19)		375 mL
2	tomatoes, cut into wedges, optional	2

A Lighter Side:
Use yogurt in place of oil; use low-fat mayonnaise and omit bacon.

1. To make dressing combine mayonnaise, vinegar, anchovies, garlic, mustard and pepper in blender or food processor. Drizzle in oil. Add cheese. Taste and adjust seasonings if necessary. (If dressing is too thick for you, thin with a little red wine vinegar and olive oil.)

2. Toss lettuce with enough dressing to coat leaves well. Sprinkle with bacon and croutons. Garnish with tomato slices.

Lentil Wild Rice Salad

This salad is as delicious as it is healthful. Use brown or white rice if you cannot find wild rice (or if the price is too high!). Use the baby green lentils if possible, as they have a nicer taste and texture. (The red lentils are better used in soups because they tend to fall apart easily.) Serve this as a side dish or as a vegetarian main course. If you are using fresh corn, try using it raw; it's perfectly crunchy and delicious.

Makes 6 to 8 servings

1 cup	wild rice	250 mL
1 cup	green lentils	250 mL
2 cups	corn niblets	500 mL
2	sweet red peppers, roasted (page 29), peeled and diced	2
1	jalapeño chile, finely chopped	1
1/2 cup	finely chopped fresh cilantro or parsley	125 mL
1/4 cup	finely chopped fresh chives or green onions	50 mL
3 oz	chèvre (goat cheese) or feta, broken up	90 g
2 tbsp	pine nuts, toasted	25 mL

DRESSING:

3 tbsp	red wine vinegar	45 mL
1	clove garlic, minced	1
1-1/2 tsp	salt	7 mL
1/2 tsp	pepper	2 mL
1/4 cup	olive oil	50 mL

1. Add rice to large pot of boiling water. Cook until tender, about 40 to 45 minutes. Drain well. Cool.

2. Rinse lentils and add to large pot of boiling water. Cook until tender, about 20 to 25 minutes. Drain well. Cool.

3. Combine rice, lentils, corn, red peppers, jalapeño, cilantro, chives, chèvre and pine nuts.

4. For the dressing, combine vinegar, garlic, salt and pepper. Whisk in oil. Taste and adjust seasonings if necessary. Toss dressing gently with salad ingredients.

Green Salad with Mustard Vinaigrette

Here's a simple green salad that is perfect as an appetizer or as a salad with or after the main course. Be sure to use the best quality when you are using only a few ingredients. You can change the tastes in this salad by using different vinegars (try raspberry, sherry or balsamic), oils (try part walnut oil or a tiny amount of sesame oil) and/or fresh herbs (such as basil, dill or cilantro).

Makes about 4 servings

2 tbsp	red wine vinegar	25 mL
1	small clove garlic, minced	1
1/2 tsp	Dijon mustard	2 mL
1/2 tsp	salt	2 mL
pinch	pepper	pinch
1/4 cup	olive oil (or to taste)	50 mL
8 cups	mixed salad greens, torn into bite-sized pieces	2 L

1. Whisk together vinegar, garlic, mustard, salt and pepper. Slowly whisk in olive oil. Taste and adjust seasonings if necessary.

2. Place salad greens in large bowl and toss well with dressing.

Chinese Chicken Salad

This is a different way to use up leftover roast turkey or chicken.
Make the salad an hour or two ahead of serving — the lettuce will
wilt, but it tastes great in this recipe. The peas and corn niblets can
be used cooked or raw.
Makes 6 to 8 servings

1	large head iceberg lettuce, chopped (about 8 cups/2 L)	1
1/2 cup	finely chopped fresh cilantro or parsley	125 mL
1/4 cup	finely chopped fresh chives or green onions	50 mL
3 cups	shredded or diced cooked chicken	750 mL
4	carrots, grated	4
1/2	English cucumber, peeled and chopped	1/2
1 cup	peas	250 mL
1 cup	corn niblets	250 mL

DRESSING:

2 tbsp	olive oil	25 mL
1 tbsp	dark sesame oil	15 mL
2 tbsp	peanut butter	25 mL
2 tbsp	soy sauce	25 mL
2 tbsp	balsamic vinegar	25 mL
1 tbsp	hoisin sauce	15 mL
1 tsp	hot chile paste, optional	5 mL
1	clove garlic, minced	1

Garnish:
Add 1/2 cup/125 mL coarsely
chopped roasted peanuts.

1. Combine the lettuce, cilantro, chives, chicken, carrots, cucumber, peas and corn.

2. Blend together olive oil, sesame oil, peanut butter, soy sauce, vinegar, hoisin sauce, chile paste and garlic.

3. Toss dressing with salad ingredients and sprinkle with peanuts. Allow to marinate for 1 to 2 hours before serving.

3 *Tortillas*

TECHNIQUES AND TIPS

- *There are basically two types of tortillas — corn and flour (wheat). Corn tortillas are used for nachos, most commercial tortilla chips, tacos, tostados and enchiladas, among other things. Flour tortillas are used for quesadillas, fajitas, burritos and chimichangas, as well as other dishes.*
- *Flour tortillas are very versatile. They can be used as the "bread" in a rolled sandwich, or as a thin, crispy pizza base. They can be fried, grilled or baked for quesadillas.*
- *Most commercial tortilla chips are deep-fried, but it is easy to make your own low-fat versions. Cut corn or flour tortillas into wedges (it is easier to use scissors than a knife) and arrange on a baking sheet in a single layer. Leave plain or brush with a little oil and sprinkle with herbs, sesame seeds and/or salt. Bake in a preheated 400°F/200°C oven for about 10 minutes, or until crisp.*
- *Tortillas are usually available in the dairy or frozen food section of the supermarket. They defrost quickly at room temperature or in the microwave.*

TECHNIQUE REVIEW

See this on the video

Spread the filling almost to the edge.

Roll the tortilla tightly.

For a pretty presentation, slice the tortilla on an angle.

The quesadilla can be sliced into triangles for an appetizer.

Be sure to prick the tortilla when using as a pizza base.

Clockwise, from left: Red Pepper and Fontina Pizza (page 29); Tortilla Roll-ups with Smoked Salmon (facing page); Chile and Cheese Quesadillas, (page 28)

Tortilla Roll-ups with Smoked Salmon Spread

See this on the video

Eat these in the roll for a hearty sandwich or slice them into pinwheels for hors d'oeuvres. You can see how beautiful these look in the video; you'll also see how to roll and slice them easily.

This salmon mixture can be served as a spread with crackers, as a filling for mushroom caps or mini pitas, or as a topping for baked potatoes. You can also make roll-ups using other filling ingredients; try spreading the tortillas with tuna salad or hummos (page 10) and top with shredded vegetables such as carrots or lettuce.

Makes 32 slices

8 oz	smoked salmon	250 g
1 tbsp	grated white horseradish	15 mL
2 tbsp	lemon juice	25 mL
1/4 tsp	pepper	1 mL
8 oz	ricotta cheese	250 g
2 tbsp	sour cream or unflavoured yogurt	25 mL
4	9-inch/23 cm flour tortillas	4
1 cup	watercress leaves, or 2 cups/500 mL shredded lettuce or raw spinach	250 mL

A Lighter Side:

Use low-fat ricotta or yogurt cheese (page 14); be sure to use yogurt instead of sour cream.

1. Cut salmon into pieces and chop in a food processor with horseradish, lemon juice and pepper.

2. Blend in ricotta. Add enough sour cream or yogurt to make a spreadable consistency.

3. Arrange tortillas on counter in a single layer. Divide salmon mixture and spread over tortillas. Top with watercress, leaving a 1-inch/2.5 cm border at the top so the roll will hold. Roll up tightly. Wrap and refrigerate until ready to serve.

4. Just before serving, trim off ends of rolls. Slice each roll into 8 pieces. Arrange on serving platter cut side up.

See this on the video

Chile and Cheese Quesadillas

Cut these quesadillas into wedges for an appetizer, or serve in halves as a main-course sandwich for lunch or a light dinner. The video shows just how these look when cooked. Use Fontina cheese, basil and diced roasted red peppers for a Mediterranean version.

Makes 16 wedges

4	9-inch/23 cm flour tortillas	4
3 cups	grated Monterey Jack cheese or medium Cheddar	750 mL
1/2 cup	diced mild green chiles	125 mL
1	jalapeño, finely diced, or other small, medium-hot green chile	1
1/2 cup	finely chopped fresh cilantro or parsley	125 mL

1. Arrange flour tortillas in a single layer on work surface.

2. Lightly toss cheese with mild chiles, jalapeño and cilantro.

3. Spread mixture over one-half of each tortilla. Fold unfilled side over filled side and press down gently.

4. Cook tortillas in lightly oiled skillet, or on grill for 2 to 3 minutes per side, or arrange in single layer on baking sheet and bake in preheated 400°F/200°C oven for 10 minutes, or until lightly browned and cheese has melted. Allow to cool for 1 to 2 minutes.

5. Cut each quesadilla into four wedges to serve as an appetizer.

A Lighter Side:

Use 2 cups/500 mL lower-fat cheese and add 2 peeled and diced roasted sweet red peppers.

Red Pepper and Fontina Pizza

See this on the video

Tortillas make a delicate thin crust for pizza, but make sure you prick them before baking, as I show on the video, so they don't puff up. Use any toppings you like or have an array of toppings and allow guests to make their own creations.

Makes four 9-inch/23 cm pizzas

4	9-inch/23 cm flour tortillas	4
4 cups	grated Fontina or mozzarella cheese	1 L
1/2 cup	tomato sauce	125 mL
2	roasted sweet red peppers, cut into large pieces	2
1/3 cup	pitted black olives	75 mL
2 tbsp	finely chopped fresh basil or parsley	25 mL

1. Prick tortillas with a fork so they will not puff too much. Arrange directly on the rack in preheated 425°F/220°C oven. Bake for 4 to 6 minutes, turning once, until crisp and lightly browned. Cool. Reduce oven temperature to 400°F/200°C.

2. Arrange tortillas on baking sheets in single layer and sprinkle with grated cheese. Dot with tomato sauce, pepper pieces, olives and half the basil.

3. Bake in 400°F/200°C oven for 10 to 12 minutes, until cheese is bubbling. Sprinkle with remaining basil before serving.

Hint:

Roasting red peppers brings out their sweet, earthy taste. Broil or barbecue the peppers on all sides until black. Cool, remove peel, discard ribs and seeds and cut up.

Hint:

To dot tomato sauce on easily, place in a squeeze bottle.

Chicken Fajitas

This dish is very popular in TexMex restaurants, but it is easy to make at home. You can add the condiments before folding up the tortilla and eat the fajita (carefully!) like a hot dog, or you can serve the fajitas with the condiments alongside, and eat them with a knife and fork.

Makes 6 servings

6	9-inch/23 cm flour tortillas	6
2 tbsp	olive oil	25 mL
12 oz	boneless, skinless chicken breasts, cut into strips	375 g
1	large onion, sliced	1
1	clove garlic, finely chopped	1
1	jalapeño chile, finely chopped	1
1	sweet red pepper, cut into strips	1
1	sweet green pepper, cut into strips	1
1/2 tsp	salt	2 mL
1/4 tsp	pepper	1 mL
1/4 cup	finely chopped fresh cilantro or parsley	50 mL

Condiments:
salsa (page 11), guacamole (page 9), sour cream or yogurt cheese (page 14), grated Monterey Jack cheese

1. Wrap tortillas in foil and warm in preheated 200°F/100°C oven for about 30 minutes while preparing filling.

2. Heat oil in large, non-stick skillet or wok. Add chicken. Stir-fry for about 3 minutes, until almost cooked through.

3. Add onion, garlic, jalapeño and sweet peppers. Cook for about 5 minutes, until vegetables soften and chicken is cooked through. Add salt, pepper and cilantro. Taste and adjust seasonings if necessary.

4. Transfer chicken mixture to platter. Allow guests to assemble their own fajitas with the warm tortillas and any condiments they like. Place filling down middle of tortilla, leaving about 2 inches/5 cm empty at bottom. Add condiments. Fold up bottom and fold in sides to cover.

Stacked Tortilla Wedges

These are easy to make and extremely delicious. Serve with plain sour cream or unflavoured yogurt or a combination of sour cream and salsa (page 11).

Makes 12 wedges

(page 11)

2 cups	grated Monterey Jack or Cheddar cheese	500 mL
4 oz	chèvre (goat cheese), crumbled	125 g
7 oz	frozen crabmeat, defrosted, picked over, squeezed dry and shredded	225 g
1	4-oz/114 mL tin diced mild green chiles	1
1/3 cup	finely chopped fresh cilantro or parsley	75 mL
1/4 cup	finely chopped fresh chives or green onions	50 mL
6	9-inch/23 cm flour tortillas	6

A Lighter Side:
Use lower-fat cheese.

1. Gently combine Monterey Jack, chèvre, crabmeat, chiles, cilantro and green onions.

2. Arrange tortillas in a single layer on work surface. Spread one-quarter of cheese mixture on each of 4 tortillas.

3. Place two filled tortillas in a single layer on baking sheet lined with parchment paper or lightly oiled foil. Arrange another filled tortilla on top of each. Top with plain tortillas. Press down gently.

4. Just before serving, bake tortillas in preheated 400°F/200°C oven for about 15 minutes, or until top browns lightly and cheese melts. Allow to cool for 5 minutes. Cut into wedges and serve with sour cream as dip.

4 Pasta

TECHNIQUES AND TIPS

- *Use lots of water when cooking pasta — at least 5 qt/5 L water per 1 lb/500 g pasta.*
- *Add about 1 tsp/5 mL salt to the pasta cooking water after it has come to the boil. Salt is not absolutely necessary (if you are watching your salt intake, don't use it), but it does season the pasta subtly.*
- *Do not add oil to the cooking water. If there is enough water in the pot, the pasta should not stick or clump. Oil leaves a slight film on the pasta and prevents the sauce from clinging properly.*
- *Pasta pots with strainer inserts are very handy. You can also use them for stock-making — just lift out the bones, meat and vegetables!*
- *When you add the pasta to the boiling water, stir it up once or twice, bring it to a boil and then lower the heat slightly so that the pasta is constantly rotating in the water but not boiling over.*

- *When you drain pasta, do not rinse it unless you are preparing pasta to use in a salad, lasagna or cannelloni dish. Rinsing stops the cooking and washes off the outside starch that thickens the sauce and helps it cling to the pasta.*
- *Taste the pasta to determine whether it is ready. It should be cooked through but not mushy.*
- *To serve pasta piping hot, cook the sauce in a large, deep skillet or Dutch oven. Toss the cooked pasta into the sauce over low heat and serve it right from the pot or a heated serving platter. The platter can be warmed by setting it over the boiling pasta. Individual plates should also be warmed, and guests should be served quickly and start eating as soon as they are served.*
- *Pasta is best served in shallow bowls, so that it doesn't sit on itself getting heavy and sticky.*

TECHNIQUE REVIEW

See this on the video

Start the tomato sauce with chopped vegetables.

Add fresh or canned tomatoes and break them up.

Use a big pot for the pasta.

The sauce can be pureed like this, or left chunky.

Mixing the pasta into the sauce helps to keep it hot.

Spaghetti with Tomato Sauce (facing page): it may be simple, but it tastes great!

Spaghetti with Tomato Sauce

See this on the video

A good version of spaghetti and tomato sauce is always popular.

Makes about 6 servings

1 tbsp	olive oil	15 mL
2	cloves garlic, finely chopped	2
1	onion, chopped	1
1/4 tsp	hot red pepper flakes, optional	1 mL
1	small carrot, chopped	1
1	small rib celery, chopped	1
1	28-oz/796 mL tin plum tomatoes, with juices	1
1/2 tsp	dried thyme	2 mL
1-1/2 tsp	salt	7 mL
1/4 tsp	pepper	1 mL
3/4 lb	spaghetti	375 g
2 tbsp	butter, optional	25 mL
1/2 cup	grated Parmesan cheese (preferably Parmigiano Reggiano)	125 mL
2 tbsp	finely chopped fresh basil or parsley	25 mL

1. Heat oil in Dutch oven or large, deep skillet. Add garlic, onion, hot pepper flakes, carrot and celery. Cook for 5 to 8 minutes, until vegetables are tender.

2. Stir in tomatoes. Bring to boil and add thyme, salt and pepper. Reduce heat and, stirring occasionally, cook uncovered for 20 minutes, or until thick.

3. Puree sauce if desired. Return sauce to pan over low heat.

4. Meanwhile, bring large pot of water to boil. Add 1 tsp/5 mL salt. Add spaghetti. Return water to boil, stir spaghetti so it doesn't stick to the bottom and cook, at a boil, until pasta is tender but not too soft.

5. Drain pasta well and add to pot with sauce. Toss gently over low heat. Add butter, cheese and basil. Taste and adjust seasonings if necessary.

Hint:
Use this sauce as the base for a meat sauce, for pizza, or anywhere tomato sauce is called for. Vary it by adding seafood, chicken and/or vegetables.

Hint:
If you do not want a spicy sauce, omit the hot pepper flakes.

Hint:
If good-flavoured fresh tomatoes are available, use about 2 lb/1 kg in place of the tinned tomatoes.

Fusilli with Scallops

This quick and elegant dish is also delicious made with linguine, spaghetti or spaghettini.

Makes about 6 servings

1 lb	fusilli	500 g
1/4 cup	olive oil	50 mL
4	cloves garlic, finely chopped	4
1/4 tsp	hot red pepper flakes	1 mL
1 lb	scallops, diced	500 g
1/3 cup	dry white wine or chicken stock	75 mL
2	tomatoes, seeded (page 11) and diced	2
1/2 tsp	pepper	2 mL
1 tsp	salt	5 mL
1/2 cup	fresh breadcrumbs, toasted	125 mL
1/4 cup	finely chopped fresh parsley	50 mL

1. Bring large pot of water to boil. Add 1 tsp/5 mL salt. Add pasta and cook for 7 to 8 minutes, or until tender.

2. Meanwhile, heat oil in large, deep skillet. Add garlic and hot pepper flakes and cook for a few minutes, but do not brown.

3. Add scallops and cook for 2 minutes. Add wine and cook for 3 minutes.

4. Stir in tomatoes, pepper and salt. Cook for 2 minutes.

5. Drain pasta well and add to skillet. Toss with sauce, breadcrumbs and parsley over low heat. Taste and adjust seasonings if necessary.

A Lighter Side:
Use half the amount of olive oil.

Hint:
To toast fresh breadcrumbs, spread on baking sheet and bake at 350°F/180°C for 10 minutes.

Spaghetti with Broccoli, Beans and Olives

This vegetarian pasta dish is as colourful as it is delicious. Rapini or Swiss chard.can be used instead of the broccoli.

Makes about 6 servings

3/4 lb	spaghetti	375 g
1	bunch broccoli, trimmed and chopped	1
1/4 cup	olive oil	50 mL
4	cloves garlic, finely chopped	4
pinch	hot red pepper flakes	pinch
4 oz	mushrooms, sliced	125 g
1 cup	cooked red kidney beans	250 mL
1 tsp	salt	5 mL
1/2 tsp	pepper	2 mL
1/2 cup	pitted black olives, chopped	125 mL
1/4 cup	finely chopped fresh parsley	50 mL

A Lighter Side:
Use half the olive oil and half the olives.

1. Bring large pot of water to boil. Add 1 tsp/5 mL salt. Add spaghetti and cook for 5 minutes. Add broccoli and cook for 5 minutes longer.

2. Meanwhile, heat oil in large, deep skillet. Add garlic and hot pepper flakes and cook gently for 3 minutes until fragrant and tender, but do not brown.

3. Add mushrooms and cook for a few minutes. Add beans, salt and pepper and cook for a few minutes longer.

4. Add olives to sauce. Heat thoroughly. Drain pasta and broccoli. Toss with sauce and parsley. Taste and adjust seasonings if necessary.

Spicy Singapore Shrimp Noodles

If you cannot find the thin rice noodles, use regular spaghettini or angel hair.

Makes 4 to 6 servings

1/2 lb	rice vermicelli	250 g
1/3 cup	chicken stock, fish stock or water	75 mL
2 tbsp	soy sauce	25 mL
1 tbsp	granulated sugar	15 mL
1 tsp	salt, optional	5 mL
2 tbsp	dark sesame oil	25 mL
1 tbsp	rice wine	15 mL
2 tbsp	vegetable oil	25 mL
12 oz	cleaned shrimp, diced	375 g
2	cloves garlic, finely chopped	2
1 tbsp	finely chopped fresh ginger root	15 mL
3	green onions, finely chopped	3
1 tbsp	curry powder	15 mL
1/2 tsp	hot chile paste, optional	2 mL
2	leeks or small onions, thinly sliced	2
1	carrot, grated	1
1	sweet red pepper, cut into thin strips	1
4 oz	bean sprouts	125 g

1. Place noodles in bowl and cover with boiling water. Allow to soak for 5 minutes. Drain well.

2. Combine stock, soy sauce, sugar, salt, sesame oil and rice wine. Reserve.

3. Heat vegetable oil in wok or large, deep skillet. Add shrimp and stir-fry for a few minutes until partially cooked. Remove from pan and reserve.

4. Add garlic, ginger and green onions to pan. Cook for 30 seconds. Add curry powder and chile paste and cook for 20 seconds.

5. Add leeks, carrot and red pepper. Cook until just wilted.

6. Add bean sprouts and sauce and bring to boil.

7. Add shrimp and noodles. Cook until noodles are tender and well combined, about 6 minutes. Taste and adjust seasonings if necessary.

5 Stir-frying
TECHNIQUES AND TIPS

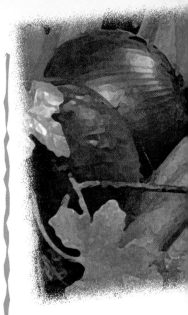

- *Be organized when you are cooking stir-fried dishes. The actual cooking should be done at the last minute, but all the preparation can be done ahead of time.*
- *Prepare and measure all your ingredients before starting. Have all sauces made and all precooking done.*
- *To slice meat or poultry very thinly, partially freeze first.*
- *Use an unflavoured cooking oil that has a high burning point. Peanut oil, soya oil, corn oil, canola oil and safflower oil are all popular oils for stir-frying.*
- *Add the ingredients that take the longest to cook first (e.g., onions or carrots) and end with the ingredients that take only seconds (e.g., snow peas or bean sprouts).*
- *Once you start to cook, cook quickly and on very high heat unless otherwise specified.*
- *Always stir up sauces, especially those containing cornstarch, before adding them to pan.*
- *Always serve food immediately after stir-frying.*
- *You do not need a wok to make good stir-fried dishes, but the sloping sides do allow you to toss ingredients more easily, and the small diameter of the base means you do not have to use much oil.*
- *Even though stir-fries may use a number of unusual bottled ingredients, once you buy them, you can use them in many other stir-fried dishes.*

TECHNIQUE REVIEW

See this on the video

Being well-organized is the secret to successful stir-frying.

If the meat is partially frozen it's easy to slice into thin pieces.

Cook the meat until it loses its pink colour, then remove it from the pan.

The broccoli is cooked briefly after the seasonings.

Add the meat again, to reheat.

Sweet and Spicy Beef and Greens (page 42) is a quick, delicious stir-fry.

See this on the video # Sweet and Spicy Beef and Greens

Instead of broccoli, you can use asparagus, green beans, Chinese cabbage or bok choy. This is also great with chicken. Serve it on rice or noodles. For all the techniques required for this recipe, and to help you with all your stir-frying, please see the video.

Makes 4 to 5 servings

12 oz	flank steak, thinly sliced on the diagonal	375 g
1 tbsp	soy sauce	15 mL
1 tbsp	cornstarch	15 mL

SAUCE:

1/2 cup	chicken stock, beef stock or water	125 mL
3 tbsp	soy sauce	45 mL
2 tbsp	rice wine	25 mL
3 tbsp	brown sugar	45 mL
2 tbsp	molasses	25 mL
1 tbsp	dark sesame oil	15 mL
1 tbsp	cornstarch	15 mL

TO COOK:

2 tbsp	vegetable oil	25 mL
3	cloves garlic, finely chopped	3
1 tbsp	chopped fresh ginger root	15 mL
5	green onions, sliced	5
1 tsp	hot chile paste	5 mL
1	bunch broccoli, trimmed and chopped	1
4 oz	snow peas, trimmed	125 g

Hint:
Freeze the flank steak for 30 minutes before using, and you will be able to cut thinner slices.

1. Combine beef with 1 tbsp/15 mL soy sauce and 1 tbsp/15 mL cornstarch. Allow to marinate while preparing other ingredients or up to overnight in the refrigerator. Reserve.

2. To make sauce, combine chicken stock, 3 tbsp/45 mL soy sauce, rice wine, brown sugar, molasses, sesame oil and 1 tbsp/15 mL cornstarch.

3. Just before serving, heat vegetable oil in wok or large, deep skillet. Add beef. Stir-fry just until beef loses its raw appearance. Remove from pan and reserve. (Add a bit more oil to pan if necessary.)

4. Add garlic, ginger, green onions and chile paste to pan. Stir-fry for 1 minute. Add broccoli. Cook for 3 to 4 minutes, just until broccoli turns bright green.

5. Stir up sauce and add to pan. Bring to boil. Cook for about 1 minute.

6. Add beef and snow peas. Toss well to heat. Taste and adjust seasonings if necessary.

Chicken Stir-fry with Teriyaki Sauce

This recipe always gets rave reviews. It's a great dish for college students in particular to have in their repertoire, because it's so easy to make. For an even simpler version, use more of one of the vegetables, such as carrots, peppers or spinach.

Makes 4 to 5 servings

1 lb	boneless, skinless chicken breasts, cut into 1-inch/ 2.5 cm cubes	500 g
1/4 cup	teriyaki sauce	50 mL
1 tbsp	cornstarch	15 mL
1 tbsp	vegetable oil	15 mL
2	cloves garlic, finely chopped	2
1 tbsp	chopped fresh ginger root	15 mL
1	onion, cut into chunks	1
1	large carrot, thinly sliced on the diagonal	1
1	sweet red pepper, cut into chunks	1
1	sweet green pepper, cut into chunks	1
10 oz	fresh spinach, trimmed and chopped	300 g

SAUCE:

1/2 cup	teriyaki sauce	125 mL
3 tbsp	water	45 mL
1 tbsp	cornstarch	15 mL
1 tbsp	cold water	15 mL
3	green onions, sliced	3

1. Combine chicken cubes with 1/4 cup/50 mL teriyaki sauce and 1 tbsp/15 mL cornstarch. Marinate for 20 minutes to 2 hours in the refrigerator.

2. Heat oil in wok or large, deep skillet. Add chicken pieces and stir-fry until lightly browned, about 2 minutes.

3. Add garlic and ginger and stir-fry for 1 minute. Add onion, carrot and peppers. Combine well.

4. Add 1/2 cup/125 mL teriyaki sauce and 3 tbsp/45 mL water. Bring to boil, reduce heat and simmer gently for 5 minutes, or until chicken is cooked through and vegetables are bright and tender. Add spinach.

5. Combine 1 tbsp/15 mL cornstarch and 1 tbsp/15 mL cold water. Add to pan and bring to a boil. Cook just until mixture thickens. Add green onions. Taste and adjust seasonings if necessary.

Noodles with Stir-fried Vegetables

These stir-fried vegetables are also great without the noodles (make half the amount of sauce). For a more substantial version you can add shrimp or chicken.

Makes 6 to 8 servings

PASTA:

1 lb	linguine	500 g
2 tbsp	dark sesame oil	25 mL

SAUCE:

1-1/2 cups	chicken stock or water	375 mL
2 tbsp	soy sauce	25 mL
2 tbsp	rice wine	25 mL
1/3 cup	oyster sauce	75 mL
1 tsp	granulated sugar	5 mL

TO COOK:

1 tbsp	vegetable oil	15 mL
3	cloves garlic, finely chopped	3
1 tbsp	chopped fresh ginger root	15 mL
4	green onions, sliced	4
10	mushrooms, preferably oyster or shiitake, sliced (about 4 oz/125 g)	10
1	carrot, grated	1
1	sweet red pepper, cut into thin strips	1
1	bunch broccoli, trimmed and chopped	1
2 tbsp	cold water	25 mL
2 tbsp	cornstarch	25 mL
1/3 cup	finely chopped fresh cilantro	75 mL

1. Bring large pot of water to boil. Add 1 tsp/5 mL salt. Add pasta and cook until tender. Drain well. Toss with sesame oil.

2. Meanwhile, for the sauce, combine chicken stock, soy sauce, rice wine, oyster sauce and sugar. Reserve.

3. To cook, heat vegetable oil in large wok or large, deep skillet or Dutch oven. Add garlic, ginger and green onions and cook for 30 seconds, until fragrant. Add mushrooms and cook for a few minutes.

4. Add carrot, red pepper and broccoli. Stir-fry for 2 minutes.

5. Add sauce and bring to boil. Cook for another 2 minutes.

6. Combine cold water and cornstarch. Add to vegetables. Stir in noodles and heat to boiling. Toss with cilantro. Taste and adjust seasonings if necessary.

6 Fish and Seafood

TECHNIQUES AND TIPS

- *When buying fresh fish, whether whole, steaks or fillets, look for fish that smells very fresh and not at all "fishy." If the fish is whole, the flesh should be fairly firm and should spring back when pressed gently. The gills should be red, the eyes clear and full and the skin smooth and moist.*
- *When buying frozen fish, look for packages that seem evenly frozen. If there is ice at one end of the package, it could be an indication that the fish has been refrozen.*
- *Always defrost fish in the refrigerator or in the microwave according to the manufacturer's directions. Do not refreeze fish.*
- *Store fresh or defrosted fish in the coldest part of your refrigerator. Remove any plastic wrapping and place the fish in a dish, covered loosely, set over a dish of ice.*
- *Use fresh or defrosted fish quickly—usually within a day or two of purchasing.*
- *The general rule for cooking fish—no matter what method (barbecuing, broiling, baking, poaching or frying)—is 10 minutes per inch/2.5 cm of thickness over medium-high or high heat.*
- *Buy 4 oz to 6 oz/125 g to 175 g per person if you are serving boneless fish fillets. Buy 6 oz to 8 oz/180 g to 250 g per person if you are serving fish steaks.*
- *Marinate fish no longer than 5 to 10 minutes if there is an acidic ingredient (e.g., citrus juice) in the marinade. If you let it sit longer, the fish will appear to "cook" and change in texture.*

TECHNIQUE REVIEW

See this on the video

Fresh fish should be firm, with no odour.

Make a steamer by using a rack set in water in a larger pan.

Put fish in a pan and set in the steamer.

Spoon the sauce over. Cover with lid or foil.

Another steamer technique: use chopsticks in the bottom of the pan.

Steamed Sea Bass in Black Bean Sauce (page 50) is one of my favourites.

See this on the video # Steamed Sea Bass
in Black Bean Sauce

Steaming is a healthful, moist cooking method. Even if you do not have a professional steamer in your kitchen, you will probably be able to improvise one, as shown on the video. If not, the fish can be covered with foil and baked at 425°F/220°C for 10 minutes, or just until it is cooked through.

Black bean sauce is made with fermented soy beans and is used in Asian dishes; Lee Kum Kee is my favourite brand.

This dish is also delicious made with salmon or halibut. Serve it with rice.

Makes 4 servings

4	6-oz/180 g sea bass or salmon fillets, about 1 inch/2.5 cm thick	4
2 tbsp	black bean sauce	25 mL
1 tbsp	dark sesame oil	15 mL
1 tbsp	chopped fresh ginger root	15 mL
1/2 tsp	pepper	2 mL
2 tbsp	frozen orange juice concentrate	25 mL
2 tbsp	water	25 mL
2	green onions, finely chopped	2
2 tbsp	finely chopped fresh cilantro or parsley	25 mL

1. Pat fish dry. Place in a single layer in an 8-inch/1.5 L square or round baking dish.

2. Combine black bean sauce, sesame oil, ginger, pepper, orange juice concentrate and water. Pour over fish.

3. Set up a steaming unit by placing crisscrossed sets of chopsticks in the bottom of a wok or by placing a small rack in the bottom of a large, deep skillet. Fill with boiling water up to the rack or chopsticks. Set dish with fish on top. Cover tightly (use foil if wok or skillet does not have a tight-fitting lid).

4. Steam fish over high heat for 10 minutes, or until just cooked. Sprinkle with green onions and cilantro.

Roasted Sesame-crusted Salmon

This technique for cooking fish — browning it for a minute on each side on direct heat and then baking it at a high temperature to finish the cooking — keeps the fish very moist. The method works well for salmon, halibut, sea bass and any flaky, thicker cut of fish. Serve this salmon with steamed rice and a salad.

Makes 6 servings

1 tbsp	honey	15 mL
1 tbsp	soy sauce	15 mL
1 tsp	honey-style mustard	5 mL
1 tsp	dark sesame oil	5 mL
1	clove garlic, minced	1
6	5-oz/150 g fillets salmon, skin and bones removed (about 1 inch/2.5 cm thick)	6
2 tbsp	sesame seeds	25 mL
1/2 tsp	salt	2 mL
1 tbsp	olive oil	15 mL

1. Combine honey, soy sauce, mustard, sesame oil and garlic. Rub into salmon. Sprinkle with sesame seeds and salt.

2. Brush large skillet (preferably non-stick with oven-safe handle) with olive oil. Heat pan and add salmon. Cook for 1 minute per side.

3. Transfer salmon to preheated 400°F/200°C oven for 7 to 8 minutes, or until fish is just cooked through. If pan cannot be used in the oven, simply transfer fish to a baking sheet lined with parchment paper and bake for about 1 minute longer than suggested above.

Seafood and Potato Casserole

Instead of baking this in one large dish, you could use individual gratin dishes. Serve this casserole with a salad and P.E.I. dinner rolls (page 82).

Makes 6 to 8 servings

1 lb	cleaned shrimp, cooked and cut into 1-inch/2.5 cm pieces	500 g
1 lb	scallops, cooked and cut in half	500 g
1 lb	thick, white-fleshed fish steak (such as halibut, haddock or cod), cooked	500 g
1 lb	potatoes, boiled and cut into 3/4-inch/2 cm chunks	500 g
1 tbsp	olive oil	15 mL
8 oz	mushrooms, sliced	250 g
1	small clove garlic, finely chopped	1
2 tbsp	butter	25 mL
1/4 cup	all-purpose flour	50 mL
2 cups	milk, hot	500 mL
2 tsp	salt	10 mL
1/2 tsp	pepper	2 mL
pinch	nutmeg	pinch
pinch	cayenne	pinch
1/2 tsp	dried tarragon, or 1 tbsp/15 mL fresh	2 mL
3 cups	grated Cheddar cheese	750 mL

A Lighter Side:
Use low-fat milk and half the cheese.

Hint:
For an upscale version of macaroni and cheese, substitute cooked pasta for the potatoes.

1. Combine shrimp, scallops and fish. Drain off any juices and reserve. Add potatoes to seafood.

2. Heat olive oil. Add mushrooms and garlic and cook until mushrooms are dry. Combine with seafood.

3. In large saucepan, melt butter. Add flour. Cook, stirring constantly, for about 3 minutes, but do not brown.

4. Whisk in hot milk, any juices from the seafood (up to a few tablespoons), salt, pepper, nutmeg, cayenne and tarragon. Bring to boil. Sauce should be very thick. (It will thin out when baked with fish and mushrooms.) Add drained seafood mixture and combine gently with sauce.

5. Spoon seafood into a buttered 12 x 8-inch/3 L casserole or baking dish and sprinkle with cheese. Bake in preheated 375°F/190°C oven for 25 to 30 minutes, until casserole is heated through and cheese has melted and become crusty. Allow casserole to rest for 10 minutes before serving.

Grilled Swordfish with Black Olive Salsa

Swordfish steaks can be thick or thin. Cook 1-inch/2.5 cm steaks for about 10 minutes, turning once; cook 1/4-inch/5 mm steaks for 3 to 4 minutes, turning once.

Makes 6 servings

6	swordfish steaks (about 6 oz/175 g each)	6
2 tbsp	lemon juice	25 mL
2 tbsp	olive oil	25 mL
1/2 tsp	salt	2 mL
1/2 tsp	pepper	2 mL
1 tbsp	finely chopped fresh rosemary, or 1/2 tsp/2 mL dried	15 mL

BLACK OLIVE SALSA:

1 cup	pitted black olives, finely chopped	250 mL
1	clove garlic, minced	1
2 tbsp	finely chopped fresh basil or parsley	25 mL
1 tbsp	balsamic vinegar	15 mL
1/2 tsp	salt	2 mL
1/4 tsp	pepper	1 mL

1. Pat fish dry.

2. Combine lemon juice, olive oil, 1/2 tsp/2 mL salt, 1/2 tsp/2 mL pepper and rosemary. Add fish to marinade and turn to coat well. Marinate for 5 to 10 minutes.

3. Combine olives, garlic, basil, vinegar, 1/2 tsp/2 mL salt and 1/4 tsp/1 mL pepper.

4. Barbecue or broil swordfish for 10 minutes per inch of thickness, turning once during cooking.

5. Serve swordfish with about 3 tbsp/45 mL salsa spread over each piece.

Hint:
Pureed, this olive salsa can also be served as an appetizer, spread on bruschetta or crackers.

A Lighter Side:
Use 3/4 cup/175 mL chopped roasted red peppers and only 1/4 cup/50 mL olives.

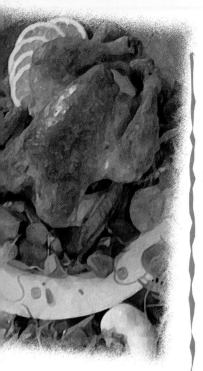

7 Chicken

TECHNIQUES AND TIPS

- *Chicken is very perishable. Use or freeze within two days of purchasing.*
- *Keep chicken refrigerated until ready to cook. If you are marinating chicken for longer than 10 minutes, refrigerate it.*
- *Thoroughly wash hands, utensils, cutting boards and plates that have been in contact with raw chicken. Although salmonella (a harmful bacteria) is killed when the chicken is cooked, the bacteria can be spread to other foods eaten raw, through improper food handling.*
- *Defrost chicken in the refrigerator or in the microwave according to the manufacturer's directions. Do not refreeze chicken.*
- *Try using ground chicken instead of ground beef in hamburgers, meatloaves and meatballs. Season the mixture a little more than usual.*
- *Dark meat takes a little longer to cook than white meat, so if you are cooking both, always test to see whether the dark meat is cooked through before you serve.*
- *White meat is very tender and lean, so be careful not to overcook, as it can easily become dry and tough.*
- *When you are cutting up a chicken, reserve (freeze) the wings, backbone, neck, etc., for stock-making.*

TECHNIQUE REVIEW

See this on the video

Roll the lemon and pierce it before putting in the cavity.

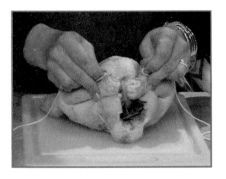

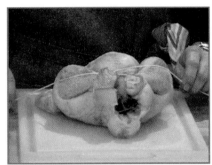

Tuck the wing tips under and begin trussing.

Tie the string tightly and brush the chicken with olive oil.

Roast breast side down first, then turn and complete cooking. Roast Chicken with Lemon and Rosemary (facing page) is simple and satisfying.

Roast Chicken with Lemon and Rosemary

See this on the video

A simple roast chicken is still one of the most delicious dinners. Because it is cooked without many flavour enhancers, it is important to buy a top-quality chicken that will have a great flavour all on its own. If you truss it, as shown on the video, the chicken can look quite important.

Makes about 4 servings

1	3-lb/1.5 kg roasting chicken	1
1	lemon	1
1/2 tsp	salt	2 mL
1/4 tsp	pepper	1 mL
2	sprigs fresh rosemary	2
4	cloves garlic, peeled	4
1 tbsp	butter or olive oil	15 mL

1. Rinse chicken inside and out and pat dry with paper towels.

2. Soften lemon (by rolling it on the counter) and pierce it in several places. Season chicken cavity with a little salt and pepper and place lemon, rosemary and garlic inside. Truss chicken with about 4 feet/1.25 m kitchen twine. (Chicken does not have to be trussed, but does look neater if it is.)

3. Rub chicken with butter or olive oil and sprinkle with remaining salt and pepper.

4. Place chicken on baking pan lined with parchment paper with the breast side down. Roast for 20 minutes in preheated 400°F/200°C oven. Turn chicken and roast for 50 minutes longer, or until it is golden brown and juices run clear when fleshy part of thigh is pierced with sharp knife.

Hint:

You can cut potatoes, sweet potatoes, onions and other root vegetables into 2-inch/5 cm chunks and roast them around the chicken.

Hint:

Parchment paper is a non-stick paper that is a valuable tool for any cook. If you don't have it, you can grease the pans or line them with greased aluminum foil.

Crispy Baked Chicken Wings

Most restaurant chicken wings have been deep-fried. But you can save fat calories by baking them instead. Serve these as an appetizer or snack with tartar sauce or chèvre dip (page 13).

Makes about 24 pieces

2 lb	chicken wings	1 kg
2 tbsp	chili powder	25 mL
2 tbsp	yellow cornmeal	25 mL
1 tsp	salt	5 mL

1. Trim off tips of chicken wings and discard or save to make stock. Separate the two remaining portions of each wing. Pat dry with paper towels.

2. Combine chili powder, cornmeal and salt. Toss with wings.

3. Line baking sheet with foil. Place rack on top. Arrange chicken wings in single layer on rack.

4. Bake in preheated 400°F/200°C oven for 45 to 55 minutes, until wings are crispy.

Spicy Grilled Chicken "Steak"

Boneless, skinless chicken breasts that have been pounded thin take only minutes to cook and are very flavourful and tender. The tender "fillet" portion of the breasts can be frozen to make chicken fingers or to use in a stir-fry. This chicken is also great hot or cold in sandwiches.

Makes 4 servings

4	boneless, skinless chicken breasts, fillets removed (about 1-1/2 lb/ 750 g total)	4
3 tbsp	olive oil	45 mL
1	clove garlic, minced	1
1 tbsp	Dijon mustard	15 mL
1/2 tsp	salt	2 mL
1/4 tsp	pepper	1 mL
1 tbsp	lemon juice	15 mL
pinch	hot red pepper flakes	pinch

1. Place each piece of chicken between two sheets of waxed paper or parchment paper. Pound chicken with a meat pounder or side of a cleaver until thin. Chicken should be about 1/2 inch/1 cm thick.

2. Combine oil, garlic, mustard, salt, pepper, lemon juice and hot pepper flakes.

3. Add chicken to marinade and turn pieces to coat well. Allow to marinate in refrigerator for 10 minutes, or up to 4 hours.

4. Heat heavy skillet, grill pan or barbecue. Brush lightly with oil. When pan is very hot, add chicken in one layer (it may have to be cooked in two pans or two batches). Cook for about 3 minutes per side, until cooked through.

Breaded Chicken Fingers

Chicken fingers can be breaded with breadcrumbs, cornmeal, cracker crumbs and even cereal crumbs!
   This dish can be served as an appetizer or main course.

Makes 4 to 5 servings

1 lb	boneless, skinless chicken breasts	500 g
1/2 cup	all-purpose flour	125 mL
2	eggs	2
2 cups	cracker crumbs (e.g., vegetable thins)	500 mL
2 tbsp	butter	25 mL
2 tbsp	vegetable oil	25 mL

1. Trim and discard any excess fat from chicken breasts. Cut chicken into pieces (you should have about 20 fingers).

2. Place flour on a flat plate or in a baking dish. Beat eggs lightly in another shallow dish and place beside the flour. Place cracker crumbs in another shallow dish beside the eggs.

3. Dredge chicken pieces with flour, shaking off excess. Dip chicken into egg, allowing excess to drip off. Then place the chicken pieces in crumbs and pat crumbs in on both sides. (Discard any excess flour, egg and crumbs.) If not cooking right away, arrange fingers in single layer on a rack set over a baking sheet. Cover loosely and refrigerate until ready to cook.

4. To cook, heat butter and oil in a large non-stick skillet. Cook chicken, in batches, until browned on both sides and cooked through, about 3 minutes per side.

A Lighter Side:

The chicken can also be baked instead of pan-fried—arrange the fingers in a single layer on an oiled baking sheet, drizzle with a little oil and bake in a preheated 400°F/200°C oven for 25 to 30 minutes, or until browned and crisp. Also, use 4 egg whites in place of 2 eggs.

Baked Chicken Breasts with Asian Barbecue Sauce

Chicken breasts are the leanest when they are cooked without the skin. They do stay much juicier, however, if they are baked on the bone. Serve this with steamed rice and stir-fried vegetables. The sauce is also great for ribs, pork chops or pork tenderloins.

Makes 6 servings

6	chicken breasts, bone in, with or without skin	6
1/4 cup	ketchup	50 mL
1/4 cup	hoisin sauce	50 mL
2 tbsp	soy sauce	25 mL
1 tbsp	rice vinegar or cider vinegar	15 mL
1 tbsp	honey	15 mL
1 tsp	Dijon mustard	5 mL
1 tsp	hot chile paste, optional	5 mL
2	cloves garlic, minced	2

1. Pat chicken breasts dry. Trim off and discard any fat.

2. Combine ketchup, hoisin sauce, soy sauce, rice vinegar, honey, mustard, chile paste and garlic. Rub into chicken breasts on both sides.

3. Arrange chicken breasts in single layer in baking dish, fleshy side up. Bake in preheated 350° F/180° C oven for 45 to 60 minues, or until chicken is cooked through but still juicy.

8 Roasting
TECHNIQUES AND TIPS

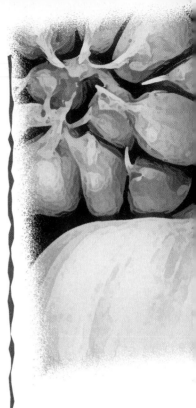

- Tender cuts of meat should be cooked using dry-heat methods —
  roasting, barbecuing, broiling, grilling or frying. Tougher cuts
  should be cooked using moist-heat methods, such as pot-roasting,
  braising or stewing.

- Roasting is a dry-heat method that cooks food relatively quickly.
  The food is baked uncovered, without liquid.

- Pot-roasting involves cooking food covered, in a liquid, for a long
  period of time to tenderize the dish. The food is often browned first.
  Braising involves the same technique using individual serving
  pieces, such as Swiss steak; stewing uses smaller pieces or cubes.

- To decide whether a cut of meat is tough or tender, ask the
  butcher to show you which part of the animal the meat is from.
  In general, the farther the meat is from the ground
  (e.g., tenderloin), the more tender it is. The closer it is to the
  ground (e.g., the shank), the tougher it is.

- When you are estimating the cooking time for a roast, consider
  the size and shape as well as the weight. A 3-lb/1.5 kg round
  roast will take longer to cook than a 3-lb/1.5 kg flattened
  butterflied leg of lamb.

- A meat thermometer takes the guesswork out of cooking a roast.
  The thin instant-read thermometers are preferable, as they are
  used when you think the meat is ready, rather than being left in
  the meat during cooking (this punctures the meat and allows the
  juices to run out). When you use a thermometer, be sure the tip is
  not touching bone or fat, or the temperature will not be accurate.

TECHNIQUE REVIEW

See this on the video

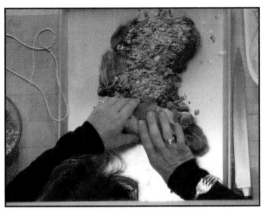

To stuff a butterflied leg of lamb, spoon on the stuffing, roll leg and tie.

Rolled Leg of Lamb with Herb Stuffing (page 66)

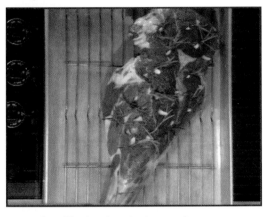

Roast a leg of lamb with garlic cloves and rosemary inserted into the meat.

Test for doneness with a meat thermometer.

To carve, hold the leg firmly with the knife edge away from you.

Roast Leg of Lamb with Rosemary and Garlic (page 64)

See this on the video

Roast Leg of Lamb with Rosemary and Garlic

This traditional way of seasoning the lamb involves cutting tiny slits in the surface of the meat and inserting flavourful rosemary and garlic.

If the leg is too long for your roasting pan, ask the butcher to cut off the end, and roast the end beside the main piece.

Makes 6 to 8 servings

6 lb	leg of lamb, bone in	3 kg
1 tbsp	olive oil	15 mL
1 tsp	salt	5 mL
1 tsp	pepper	5 mL
5	cloves garlic, cut into slivers	5
16	tiny sprigs fresh rosemary	16
1 tbsp	honey	15 mL
1 tbsp	water	15 mL

1. Trim lamb of all visible fat and rub with olive oil, salt and pepper.

2. Cut about 16 slits in the surface of lamb and insert garlic sliver and sprig of rosemary into each.

3. Place lamb on rack in roasting pan. Roast, uncovered, in preheated 425°F/220°C oven for 20 minutes. Reduce heat to 375°F/190°C and continue to roast for another 55 minutes for rare — 130°F/55°C on a meat thermometer. (Roast 10 to 15 minutes longer for medium.)

4. About 15 minutes before end of cooking time, combine honey and water. Brush over lamb.

5. Allow lamb to rest for 10 minutes before carving. To carve, hold leg up by the bone and carve the meat off the bone. Keep rotating the leg to reach all the meat.

Butterflied Leg of Lamb with Apricot Glaze

This is the quickest way to roast lamb, and it is delicious, too. Although this roast weighs 3 lb/1.5 kg, it doesn't take long to cook because it is flat and thin. The meat can also be barbecued for about 10 minutes per side. Serve it with couscous.

Makes about 8 servings

3 lb	butterflied leg of lamb	1.5 kg
1/4 cup	apricot jam	50 mL
2 tbsp	hoisin sauce	25 mL
1 tbsp	Dijon mustard	15 mL
1 tbsp	lemon juice	15 mL
1 tbsp	minced fresh ginger root	15 mL
2	cloves garlic, minced	2
1 tbsp	Worcestershire sauce	15 mL

1. Trim any excess fat from lamb.

2. Combine apricot jam, hoisin sauce, mustard, lemon juice, ginger, garlic and Worcestershire sauce. Rub into lamb.

3. Place lamb on baking sheet lined with parchment paper. Roast, uncovered, in preheated 425°F/220°C oven for 10 minutes. Reduce heat to 375°F/190°C and roast for 15 to 20 minutes longer, or until a meat thermometer registers 130°F/55°C for rare.

See this on the video

Rolled Leg of Lamb with Herb Stuffing

If a leg of lamb is boned out and spread flat, it will roast very quickly. But if the same piece of meat is rolled up, and its thickness is doubled or tripled, then the roasting time will increase, even if the weight is the same. The method for stuffing and rolling is shown on the video.

Serve this with scalloped potatoes (page 75).

Makes about 8 servings

3 lb	butterflied leg of lamb	1.5 kg
1 tsp	salt	5 mL
1 cup	fresh breadcrumbs	250 mL
1/4 cup	finely chopped fresh parsley	50 mL
1/4 cup	finely chopped fresh chives or green onions	50 mL
1 tbsp	finely chopped fresh rosemary, or 1/2 tsp/2 mL dried	15 mL
1	clove garlic, minced	1
1 tbsp	olive oil	15 mL
1/2 tsp	pepper	2 mL

GLAZE:

2 tbsp	Dijon mustard	25 mL
2 tbsp	honey	25 mL
2	cloves garlic, minced	2
2 tbsp	finely chopped fresh rosemary, or 1 tsp/5 mL dried	25 mL

1. Trim any excess fat from lamb. Arrange flat on work surface with the boned side up. Sprinkle with salt.

2. Combine breadcrumbs, parsley, chives, 1 tbsp/15 mL rosemary, 1 minced clove garlic, olive oil and pepper. Spread over surface of lamb.

3. Roll up meat tightly along short side and tie securely with kitchen twine.

4. Combine mustard, honey, 2 minced cloves garlic and 2 tbsp/15 mL rosemary. Rub all over surface of lamb.

5. Place lamb on rack set in baking dish. Roast, uncovered, in preheated 400°F/200°C oven for 15 minutes. Reduce heat to 350°F/180°C and continue to roast for 35 to 45 minutes, or until meat thermometer registers 130°F/55°C for rare. (Roast 15 minutes longer for medium.) Allow roast to rest for 5 to 10 minutes before carving into slices.

Pork Tenderloin with Apple Thyme Glaze

Overcooked pork is dry and tough, so these tenderloins should be just cooked through. The glaze is also great with a butterflied leg of lamb.

Makes about 6 servings

2 lb	pork tenderloin	1 kg
1 tbsp	Dijon mustard	15 mL
1 tsp	dried thyme, or	5 mL
	2 tbsp/25 mL fresh	
1 tsp	salt	5 mL
1/2 tsp	pepper	2 mL
1	clove garlic, minced	1
1/4 cup	apple jelly	50 mL

1. Pat pork dry.

2. Combine mustard, thyme, salt, pepper, garlic and apple jelly. Rub into pork.

3. Place pork on a rack set in roasting pan. Roast, uncovered, in preheated 375°F/190°C oven for 35 to 45 minutes or until pork is just cooked through — 160°F/70°C on a meat thermometer. Meat should still be juicy.

Roast Prime Rib of Beef

Prime rib is the best cut of beef for roasting, but you could also use a sirloin tip or strip loin roast. This recipe is very easy, and the "rub" can be used with any tender cut. Do not worry about the quantity of garlic — it will become soft and sweet-tasting when cooked.

Makes about 8 servings

2	heads garlic, separated into cloves but not peeled	2
1 tbsp	Dijon mustard	15 mL
2 tsp	salt, divided	10 mL
1 tsp	pepper	5 mL
5 tbsp	olive oil, divided	75 mL
3 lb	prime rib roast, bone in	1.5 kg
2 lb	potatoes, peeled or scrubbed and cut into 1-1/2-inch/4 cm pieces	1 kg

1. Place garlic cloves in single layer on baking sheet. Roast in preheated 350°F/180°C oven for 20 to 30 minutes, or until garlic is tender and cooked through. Cool and peel.

2. Mash garlic in blender or food processor and combine with mustard, 1 tsp/5 mL salt, pepper and 3 tbsp/45 mL olive oil.

3. Rub garlic mixture all over roast. Allow to marinate for 30 minutes at room temperature or longer in the refrigerator.

4. Toss potatoes with remaining 2 tbsp/25 mL olive oil and 1 tsp/5 mL salt.

5. Place roast, bone side down, in oiled roasting pan. Arrange potatoes around meat.

6. Cook, uncovered, in preheated 425°F/220°C oven for 10 minutes. Lower heat to 350°F/180°C and continue roasting until a meat thermometer reaches 130°F/55°C — about 1 hour for rare. Allow roast to rest for 10 minutes before carving.

9 Potatoes

TECHNIQUES AND TIPS

- There are many different varieties of potatoes, and some are used for specific purposes. Baking potatoes have a higher starch content, so they cook up dry and fluffy; boiling potatoes are moister and waxy when cooked. Idaho, russets and Yukon gold potatoes are great for baking, roasting, mashing, frying, gratins, pancakes and soups (some people like to use Yukon golds because they look as though they have butter in them!). New potatoes are perfect for boiling and potato salads.

- When you boil potatoes or other root vegetables, always start with cold water. Cut the potatoes into same-sized pieces so they cook evenly.

- It is better to peel and cut potatoes just before cooking, but if you must prepare them ahead of time, cover them with cold water to prevent discoloration.

- Store potatoes at room temperature rather than in the refrigerator. Remove them from plastic bags to help prevent them from becoming damp and rotten.

- Potatoes with a greenish tinge can taste bitter and may not have been properly stored. Be sure to cut out any sprouts before using the potatoes.

- Most potato dishes do not freeze well, as the potatoes can easily become watery.

TECHNIQUE REVIEW

See this on the video

Start potatoes in cold water.

To make mashed potatoes light and fluffy, the liquid you add must be hot.

Mix in the seasonings and serve immediately or prepare for baking later.

Mashed potatoes can be made ahead and piped into a baking dish.

Sprinkle with paprika before baking.

Old-fashioned Mashed Potatoes (page 72)—great comfort food!

See this on the video

Old-fashioned Mashed Potatoes

Mashed potatoes are the ultimate comfort food.

You'll see on the video that I like to mash potatoes in a food mill, but you can also use a potato ricer or potato masher. Never use a food processor, however, or your potatoes may become gluey.

Mashed potatoes taste best eaten as soon as they are ready, but if you want to make them ahead, pipe or spoon them into a buttered gratin or baking dish, brush lightly with melted butter or olive oil, dust with paprika and reheat at 350°F/180°C for 30 minutes, or until thoroughly heated.

Makes 4 to 6 servings

2 lb	potatoes (preferably russet or Yukon gold)	1 kg
2-1/2 tsp	salt, divided	12 mL
1/4 tsp	pepper	1 mL
1/4 cup	butter or olive oil	50 mL
1/2 cup	milk, hot	125 mL
1/4 cup	finely chopped fresh chives or green onions	50 mL

1. Peel potatoes and cut into 2-inch/5 cm pieces.

2. Place potatoes in saucepan and cover with cold water. Add 1 tsp/5 mL salt. Bring to a boil and cook gently, covered, for 30 minutes, or until tender. Drain well.

3. Mash potatoes with remaining 1-1/2 tsp/7 mL salt (or to taste), pepper, butter and enough hot milk to make a thick, creamy consistency. Beat in chives or green onions.

Hint:

If you like creamy, smooth potatoes, make sure the liquid you add is hot. You may have to add more or less depending on the starch content of the potatoes.

A Lighter Side:

Omit or halve the butter or oil; use low-fat milk or buttermilk, or some of the hot potato-cooking water.

Roast Potatoes with Rosemary

These potatoes go well with any roasted or grilled meat. Make any leftover roast potatoes into potato salad by tossing them with your favourite dressing.

Makes 4 to 6 servings

2 lb	baking potatoes, scrubbed and peeled	500 g
3 tbsp	olive oil	45 mL
2	cloves garlic, minced	2
1 tsp	salt	5 mL
1/2 tsp	pepper	2 mL
2 tbsp	finely chopped fresh rosemary, or 1 tsp/5 mL dried	25 mL

1. Cut potatoes into 2-inch/5 cm pieces.

2. Combine oil, garlic, salt, pepper and rosemary. Toss with potatoes.

3. Spread potatoes in single layer on baking sheet lined with parchment paper.

4. Roast in preheated 400°F/200°C oven for 50 to 55 minutes, or until potatoes are crisp on the outside and tender inside. Stir halfway through roasting time.

Accordion Chili-rubbed Baked Potatoes

The flavour of the chili oil penetrates deep into the potatoes when they are baked this way. You could also use curry powder instead of the chili powder, or use the rosemary mixture used in the roast potatoes (page 73).

Makes 4 servings

1/4 cup	olive oil	50 mL
1 tbsp	chili powder	15 mL
1 tsp	salt	5 mL
4	baking potatoes	4
	(8 oz/250 g each), well scrubbed	

1. Combine olive oil, chili powder and salt.

2. Place potatoes on cutting board. Without slicing right through, cut deep slits across potatoes every 3/4 inch/2 cm. Leave potatoes attached at the bottom. (If you put a wooden spoon alongside the potato, it will stop you from cutting right through.)

3. Arrange potatoes in single layer in baking dish and drizzle flavoured oil over top, allowing it to drip between slices.

4. Bake in preheated 400°F/200°C oven for 80 minutes, or until potatoes are cooked through and very tender.

Scalloped Potatoes with Herbed Cheese

Use baking potatoes in this recipe; the starch of the potatoes will help to thicken the milk.

Makes 4 to 6 servings

A Lighter Side:
Use low-fat milk and low-fat cream cheese.

2 cups	milk	500 mL
8 oz	cream cheese with garlic and herbs	250 g
1/2 tsp	hot red pepper sauce	2 mL
1 tsp	salt	5 mL
1/4 tsp	pepper	1 mL
pinch	nutmeg	pinch
5	medium baking potatoes (1-1/2 lb/750 g in total), peeled	5
1/4 cup	grated Parmesan cheese (preferably Parmigiano Reggiano)	50 mL

1. Blend together milk, cream cheese, hot pepper sauce, salt, pepper and nutmeg. Heat gently for 5 minutes.

2. Slice potatoes very thinly. Layer potatoes and sauce alternately in buttered 9-inch/2.5 L gratin or baking dish, ending with sauce. Sprinkle with Parmesan cheese.

3. Bake in preheated 350°F/180°C oven for 60 to 80 minutes, or until potatoes are tender when pierced with tip of a knife. Let stand for 5 to 10 minutes before serving.

10 Bread

TECHNIQUES AND TIPS

- *It is very exciting to make your first loaf of bread, and it is not at all difficult. Just remember to keep your ingredients and the environment nice and cosy, so that nothing becomes too hot (which could kill the yeast and prevent the bread from rising) or too cold (which would slow down the action of the yeast).*

- *Although you can buy yeast in different forms, these recipes use the traditional dry variety that you proof in a little sugared water. If you do not bake bread often, use the handy pre-measured envelopes. If you make bread frequently, you may want to buy yeast in tins or in bulk (1 tbsp/15 mL equals one envelope).*

- *If you use a 2 cup/500 mL glass measuring cup to dissolve the yeast in the water, you can easily see when it has bubbled up and doubled in volume.*

- *You can use a thermometer to test that the water and other liquids you are using are not hotter than 115°F/45°C, or just feel the water — if it is too hot for your hand, it is too hot for the yeast.*

- *It is always easier to make a sticky dough and then add extra flour than to make a dry dough and add more liquid. Therefore it is a good idea to start with less flour than the recipe lists, and add a little at a time until the consistency is right. The best bread dough contains just enough flour that it won't stick to your hands while kneading.*

- *Try to find a nice warm place for the bread to rise, but be sure it isn't too hot. The top of a refrigerator or television is usually a good location. If the spot is too hot to rest your hand on, it is too hot for the bread. You can also let the dough rise in the refrigerator overnight if you do not want to bake it until the next day. Or you can freeze the dough. In both cases, bring the dough to room temperature before baking.*

- *Bread machines that mix, knead, rise, punch down and bake the bread are terrific, but they do not allow for the hands-on contact that most people who truly love baking bread enjoy. On the other hand, it is lovely to be able to wake up to the aroma of bread baking in your kitchen.*

- *It is a shame to throw out good bread. Use leftovers to make bruschetta, croutons (page 19) or breadcrumbs.*

- *Bread dough can be kneaded by hand, in a heavy-duty mixer fitted with a dough hook, or in a food processor (follow the manufacturer's directions).*

TECHNIQUE REVIEW

See this on the video

Sprinkle the yeast on the warm water and set aside.

After 10 minutes, stir the yeast before adding it to other ingredients.

Add the stirred yeast to the other liquids.

Add the liquid ingredients to the dry, and stir.

Stir until the dough no longer sticks to the bowl, then turn it out and knead.

Put the dough in an oiled bowl and set in a warm place to rise.

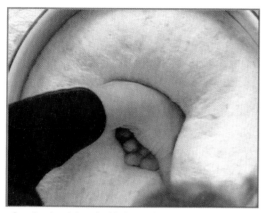

After the dough has doubled, punch it down.

Turn the dough out and pat or roll into a rectangle.

Fold the dough into thirds.

Roll it up on the short side.

Place the dough in a buttered loaf pan to rise again.

Whole Wheat Buttermilk Bread (page 80) shaped into a loaf or rolls.

See this on the video

Whole Wheat Buttermilk Bread

Watch the video on this and you'll have the confidence to try bread-making! This bread freezes well and makes fabulous toast. It can be baked in one large 9 x 5-inch/2 L loaf or two smaller 8 x 4-inch/ 1.5 L loaves. The dough can also be used to make rolls. Shape them as for dinner rolls (page 82)—you should have enough for twelve rolls.

Makes 1 large loaf

1 tsp	granulated sugar	5 mL
1/4 cup	warm water	50 mL
1	envelope dry yeast	1
1-1/2 cups	hard whole wheat flour	375 mL
1-1/2 cups	all-purpose flour (or more)	375 mL
1/4 cup	wheat bran	50 mL
1/4 cup	yellow cornmeal	50 mL
1 tsp	salt	5 mL
1 cup	buttermilk or unflavoured yogurt	250 mL
2 tbsp	vegetable oil	25 mL
3 tbsp	honey	45 mL

GLAZE:

1	egg	1
1/2 tsp	salt	2 mL

1. Dissolve sugar in warm water and sprinkle yeast over top. Allow mixture to bubble up and double in volume, about 10 minutes.

2. Meanwhile, stir together whole wheat flour, 1 cup/250 mL all-purpose flour, wheat bran, cornmeal and 1 tsp /5 mL salt.

3. Combine buttermilk, oil and honey. Warm mixture slightly, but no hotter than 115°F/45°C.

4. When yeast is ready, stir it down and combine with buttermilk mixture.

5. Stir liquid ingredients into flour mixture and add additional all-purpose flour until you have a soft dough that does not stick to your hands.

6. Knead dough on floured work surface for 10 minutes (or use a heavy-duty mixer or food processor and follow manufacturer's directions).

7. Place dough in buttered or oiled bowl. Turn dough to coat well and cover with plastic wrap and tea towel. Allow to rise in a warm spot until doubled in bulk, about 1 to 1-1/2 hours.

8. Punch dough down and shape into loaf. Place in buttered 9 x 5-inch/2 L loaf pan. Allow to rise until doubled again, about another hour.

9. Combine egg with 1/2 tsp/2 mL salt and brush over top of loaf. Bake in preheated 375°F/190°C oven for 45 minutes. Remove from pans and cool on wire racks.

Prince Edward Island Dinner Rolls

Wherever you eat in Prince Edward Island, they seem to serve these light, tender rolls! They are always made with white flour, but you could use half whole wheat for a nuttier, coarser texture.

Makes 12 rolls

1 tsp	granulated sugar	5 mL
1/4 cup	warm water	50 mL
1	envelope dry yeast	1
1 cup	milk	250 mL
2 tbsp	butter	25 mL
3 tbsp	granulated sugar	45 mL
1-1/2 tsp	salt	7 mL
1	egg	1
3 cups	all-purpose flour (or more)	750 mL

1. Dissolve 1 tsp/5 mL sugar in warm water. Sprinkle yeast over top. Allow mixture to rest for 10 minutes, or until yeast bubbles up and doubles in volume.

2. While yeast is rising, warm milk with butter, 3 tbsp/45 mL sugar and salt just until butter melts. Mixture should be just warm. Beat in egg.

3. When yeast has risen, combine with warm milk mixture.

4. Place 3 cups/750 mL flour in large bowl. Add yeast/milk mixture. Stir until a sticky dough is formed. Add enough additional flour, a little at a time, until dough is smooth and moist but not sticky.

5. Transfer dough to floured work surface and knead until dough is smooth and elastic, about 10 minutes (or use heavy-duty mixer or food processor and follow manufacturer's directions).

6. Place dough in lightly buttered or oiled bowl and turn to coat well. Cover with plastic wrap and then a tea towel. Set in a warm place to rise for about 1 to 2 hours, or until dough doubles in size.

7. Meanwhile, butter 12 regular-sized muffin cups (preferably a non-stick muffin pan).

8. When dough is ready, punch down and knead lightly. Divide into 12 equal pieces. Cut each piece in half and roll into a ball.

9. Place two balls in each muffin cup. Cover loosely with lightly buttered or oiled plastic wrap and set in warm place to rise for 30 to 45 minutes, or until rolls double in size.

10. Remove plastic wrap and bake rolls in preheated 350°F/180°C oven for about 20 minutes, or until puffed and golden brown. Remove from pans and cool on racks.

Cinnamon Buns

*Homemade cinnamon buns are almost too good to be true. Freeze
half for another time, if you can resist eating them!*

*It is important to remove the buns from the pan right after they
have baked, so that the delicious gooey syrup in the bottom will not
stick! If you really want to gild the lily, make an icing-sugar glaze
and drizzle over the top of the buns.*

Makes about 18 buns

1 tsp	granulated sugar	5 mL
1/4 cup	warm water	50 mL
1	envelope dry yeast	1
1 cup	milk	250 mL
1/4 cup	butter	50 mL
1/2 cup	granulated sugar	125 mL
1/2 tsp	salt	2 mL
2	eggs	2
5 cups	all-purpose flour (or more)	1.25 L

FILLING AND TOPPING:

1/2 cup	butter, soft	125 mL
2 cups	brown sugar	500 mL
1 tbsp	cinnamon	15 mL

1. Dissolve 1 tsp/5 mL sugar in warm water. Sprinkle yeast
over top. Allow to stand for 10 minutes. The yeast should
bubble up and double in volume.

2. Meanwhile, warm milk with butter, 1/2 cup/125 mL sugar
and salt. Stir until butter melts and sugar dissolves. Cool until
mixture feels just warm (not hot!) to the touch. Beat in eggs.

3. When yeast has doubled and milk is just warm, combine
the two mixtures.

A Lighter Side:
Use half the amount of butter
in dough, filling and topping.
Omit eggs; omit the optional
glaze.

4. Place 3 cups/750 mL flour in large bowl. Add liquid mixture and stir until mixture forms sticky dough. Add flour until the dough is smooth and moist but not sticky.

5. Knead dough on floured work surface until smooth and elastic, about 10 minutes (or use heavy-duty mixer or food processor, following manufacturer's instructions).

6. Place dough in large oiled or buttered bowl. Turn dough to coat well. Cover with plastic wrap and place tea towel over top. Allow dough to rise in warm place for 1 to 1-1/2 hours, or until doubled in size.

7. While dough is rising, generously butter two 9-inch/2.5 L baking dishes, using about 2 tbsp/25 mL soft butter in each.

8. Combine brown sugar and cinnamon and sprinkle about 1/2 cup/125 mL of this mixture in bottom of each pan.

9. Punch dough down and divide in half. Roll out each half into a large rectangle — about 12 x 14 inches/30 x 36 cm. Spread each with half the remaining soft butter. Sprinkle each with half the remaining brown sugar/cinnamon mixture. Roll up each rectangle lengthwise like a long jelly roll. Cut each into about 9 slices — about 1-1/2 inches/4 cm each.

10. Place buns, cut sides up, in prepared pans. Cover with lightly buttered plastic wrap and allow to rise in a warm place until doubled in size, 45 to 60 minutes.

11. Remove plastic wrap and bake buns in preheated 350°F/180°C for 30 to 40 minutes, until puffed and golden.

12. Invert buns onto two trays. If any of the sugar mixture sticks to the pans, scrape it out with a spoon and spread on the buns.

Pizza

Pizza dough is really just a plain bread dough that has been rolled out and not given much of a chance to rise again before being baked.

Makes two 8-inch/22 cm pizzas

1 tsp	granulated sugar	5 mL
1 cup	warm water, divided	250 mL
1	envelope dry yeast	1
3 cups	all-purpose flour (or more)	750 mL
1 tsp	salt	5 mL
1 tbsp	olive oil	15 mL
1/2 cup	thick tomato sauce	125 mL
3 cups	grated mozzarella cheese	750 mL
1/4 cup	finely chopped fresh basil, oregano or parsley	50 mL

1. Dissolve sugar in 1/2 cup/125 mL warm water. Sprinkle yeast over top and allow to rest for 10 minutes. Mixture should bubble up and double in volume.

2. Meanwhile, stir flour with salt. When yeast has bubbled, stir it down and add remaining 1/2 cup/125 mL water and olive oil.

3. Place 2 cups/500 mL flour in large bowl and add liquid. Mix dough first with wooden spoon and then with your hands. Dough will be very sticky. Add additional flour until dough is soft but not sticky. Knead dough for 5 to 10 minutes on lightly floured work surface.

4. Place dough in oiled bowl, cover with plastic wrap and tea towel and allow to rise in warm spot for about 1 hour. Dough should double in volume.

5. Punch dough down and divide in two. Roll out each circle into a thin round and place on oiled baking pan (or make one large rectangular pizza).

6. Spread each round with sauce, sprinkle with cheese and dot with basil.

7. Bake on bottom shelf of preheated 425°F/220°C oven for 15 to 20 minutes, or until crust is crisp, cheese has melted and top is lightly browned.

Hint:

You can choose different cheeses such as chèvre or gorgonzola for this pizza, or add black or green olives, anchovies or capers, hot peppers or sweet peppers, pepperoni or cooked bacon, or any other toppings of your choice.

Hint:

If you like a really thin crust, roll out the dough until it is very thin, top it and bake it quickly! If you prefer a thicker crust, roll it out, top it leisurely and leave it for about 5 minutes before baking.

A Lighter Side:

Use half the cheese.

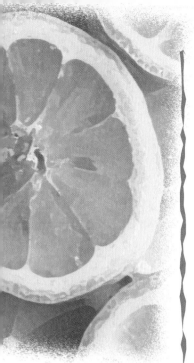

11 *Phyllo*

TECHNIQUES AND TIPS

- *Phyllo pastry is generally available frozen (some doughs fall apart more easily than others — Krinos is a good brand to buy). Defrost the package in the refrigerator overnight and then allow to stand at room temperature for 1 hour before opening.*
- *Remove phyllo from the package and lay out on a work surface. Cover immediately with a damp tea towel. Any dough you will not be using should be wrapped well and returned to the freezer, or it can be refrigerated for up to 1 month.*
- *Be organized and work quickly so that the phyllo doesn't dry out.*
- *When you want to cut back on the quantity of butter, add a bit of water to it — the proportion should be about 3 tbsp/45 mL water for 1/2 cup/125 mL melted butter.*
- *Phyllo pastry can be used in place of pizza crusts, pie crusts, turnover pastry, tart shells, strudel pastry and even spring roll wrappers or tortillas.*
- *Phyllo pastries freeze well either baked or unbaked. Freeze on a waxed paper-lined baking sheet and then store in plastic bags. Bake from the frozen state to keep the dough from becoming soggy. Bake at 400°F/200°C for 20 to 30 minutes, until crisp and hot.*

TECHNIQUE REVIEW

See this on the video

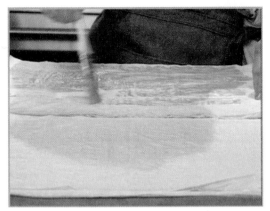

Brush each layer of phyllo with melted butter.

Cut the layered sheets into six pieces to make tarts.

Take each piece and rotate sheets of phyllo slightly.

Press firmly into non-stick muffin pan.

The baked phyllo tart is ready for filling.

Icing sugar is the final touch to Phyllo Tarts with Lemon Cream and Berries (page 90).

For Spanakopita (page 92) cut the phyllo into strips.

Put a small amount of filling into corner of strip.

Fold phyllo over filling at end, and then lengthwise.

Fold it like this.

Then start to fold it as if it were a flag.

The folded triangles have been brushed with butter or oil and then baked.

See this on the video

Phyllo Tarts with Lemon Cream and Berries

Any kind of fresh berries, or a mixture, will work well on these lovely tarts. As discussed on the video, these phyllo tarts are also wonderful with other fillings, like fruit mousse, ice cream, sherbet or fruit.

Makes 12 tarts

12	sheets phyllo pastry	12
1/2 cup	butter, melted	125 mL
1/4 cup	granulated sugar	50 mL

FILLING:

1/2 cup	lemon juice	125 mL
1 tbsp	finely grated lemon peel	15 mL
1/2 cup	granulated sugar	125 mL
2 tbsp	butter	25 mL
3	eggs	3
1 cup	whipping cream	250 mL
2 cups	fresh berries	500 mL
	Icing sugar	
	Sprigs of fresh mint	

1. Keep phyllo pastry covered with damp tea towel while you work with one sheet at a time. Arrange one sheet on work surface. Brush with melted butter and sprinkle with a bit of sugar. Make layers with five more sheets, brushing and sprinkling each layer. Make second stack of layers with remaining phyllo (keep first stack covered so it doesn't dry out).

A Lighter Side:

Use half the butter for the phyllo cups and fill tarts with sweetened yogurt cheese (page 14), fruit sorbet or fresh fruit salad.

2. With sharp knife, cut each stack of phyllo into six 6-inch/15 cm squares (approx.). Place each square in lightly buttered regular-sized muffin cup pan and press in firmly. (You can rotate pastry layers slightly so that instead of four corners there will be many points.) Repeat until you have 12 tarts. (Dough will stick up and look a bit wild.)

3. Place muffin pan on baking sheet. Bake in preheated 350°F/180°C oven for about 15 to 18 minutes, until brown and crisp. Cool.

4. Meanwhile, make filling. Place lemon juice, peel, sugar and butter in saucepan and bring to boil. Remove from heat.

5. Whisk eggs and add hot mixture to eggs off heat. Return filling to saucepan and return to heat. Stirring constantly, bring mixture to boil to thicken. Transfer to bowl and cool.

6. Whip cream until light. Fold into cold lemon mixture. Spoon into cooled tart shells.

7. Arrange berries on top. Sift a bit of icing sugar over top and garnish with mint.

See this on the video

Spanakopita (Phyllo Triangles)

This traditional Greek appetizer is one of the best. As you can see in the video, folding these triangles is not at all difficult. The triangles can be made ahead and frozen either before or after baking.

Makes about 48 triangles

1 lb	fresh spinach, well cleaned	500 g
2 tbsp	butter or olive oil	25 mL
1	small onion, finely chopped	1
1	clove garlic, finely chopped	1
8 oz	feta cheese, crumbled	250 g
2	eggs, lightly beaten	2
2 tbsp	finely chopped fresh dill	25 mL
1/4 tsp	nutmeg	1 mL
1/4 tsp	pepper	1 mL
1 lb	phyllo pastry	500 g
1/2 cup	butter, melted	125 mL
1/4 cup	fine breadcrumbs	50 mL

1. Place spinach in pot of boiling water and cook for 30 to 60 seconds, until just wilted. Drain, rinse with cold water and squeeze out any excess moisture with your hands or in a tea towel. Chop and reserve.

2. Melt butter in large, deep skillet. Cook onion and garlic until tender, but do not brown. Add spinach and cook, stirring, just until well combined.

3. Transfer mixture to bowl and cool. Stir in feta, eggs, dill, nutmeg and pepper. Reserve.

A Lighter Side:

Use 1 tbsp/15 mL olive oil in filling. Use 4 egg whites instead of 2 whole eggs. Use half the amount of butter to roll up triangles and use olive oil in place of butter to brush folded pastries.

Hint:

You can use chopped frozen spinach instead of fresh. Defrost and squeeze out any excess moisture.

4. Unwrap pastry and cut into four equal pieces crosswise. Cover with damp tea towel. Have melted butter, breadcrumbs, pastry brush and two ungreased baking sheets beside your work surface.

5. Remove one or two strips of phyllo at a time. keep the rest covered. Strips should be about 12 x 4 inches/30 x 10 cm. Brush strips with butter and dust with breadcrumbs.

6. Place teaspoonful of filling on bottom righthand side of short end of strip. Fold the bottom up to cover filling and fold the unfilled lefthand side over filling to encase it completely.

7. Fold up pouch of filling as if you were folding a flag—first to the left, then up, then to the right—to form triangles. Brush with butter. Place on baking sheet. Repeat until all filling is used.

8. Bake triangles in preheated 400°F/200°C oven for 18 to 20 minutes, or until nicely browned.

Moroccan Spiced Lamb "Cigars"

These log-shaped appetizers have a mysterious Middle Eastern flavour. They can also be made with ground chicken or ground beef.

Makes about 36 rolls

1 tbsp	olive oil	15 mL
1	small onion, chopped	1
2	cloves garlic, finely chopped	2
1 tsp	ground cumin	5 mL
1 tsp	paprika	5 mL
1/4 tsp	cayenne	1 mL
1 lb	ground lamb	500 g
1/2 cup	tomato sauce	125 mL
1	egg	1
1 tbsp	honey	15 mL
1 tsp	salt	5 mL
1/2 cup	fresh breadcrumbs	125 mL
1 lb	phyllo pastry	500 g
1/2 cup	butter, melted	125 mL
1/4 cup	sesame seeds	50 mL

A Lighter Side:

Use half the butter or use olive oil instead. Omit sesame seeds. Be sure lamb is lean or use chicken instead. Use 2 egg whites in place of whole egg.

1. Heat oil, add onion and garlic and cook until tender. Add cumin, paprika and cayenne. Cook for 30 seconds.

2. Add lamb and cook until completely coloured. Add tomato sauce and cook until mixture is very thick.

3. Add egg, honey, salt and breadcrumbs. Mix together well. Cool.

4. Take phyllo out of package and cut into thirds crosswise so that each strip is about 12 x 5 inches/30 x 12 cm. Cover with damp tea towel.

5. Work with one or two strips of phyllo at a time. Place phyllo strips on work surface and brush with butter.

6. Form 1 tbsp/15 mL filling into narrow log about 3 inches/7.5 cm long and place near bottom of short end of strip in middle.

7. Fold both sides of pastry over filling to cover it, brush pastry with butter and roll up tightly. Brush rolls with butter and sprinkle with sesame seeds. As pastries are ready, place on ungreased baking sheet.

8. Bake in preheated 400°F/200°C oven for 25 minutes, until pastries are crisp and browned.

Potato and Mushroom Strudel

This can be served as a vegetarian main course or as a side dish with roast chicken.

Makes 8 to 10 servings

6 oz	bacon, diced (6 strips), optional	180 g
1	onion, sliced	1
8 oz	mushrooms, sliced	250 g
2 lb	baking potatoes, peeled and thinly sliced	1 kg
1 tsp	salt	5 mL
1 tsp	pepper	5 mL
2 tsp	finely chopped fresh thyme, or 1/2 tsp/2 mL dried	10 mL
2 tsp	finely chopped fresh rosemary, or 1/2 tsp/2 mL dried	10 mL
1/4 cup	milk or chicken stock	50 mL
12	sheets phyllo pastry	12
1/3 cup	butter, melted (or more)	75 mL
1/4 cup	dry breadcrumbs	50 mL

1. Cook bacon until crisp. Drain on paper towels and reserve.

2. Discard all but 1 tbsp/15 mL fat from pan. Add onion and cook for a few minutes just until wilted. Add mushrooms and cook until mushrooms are tender and any excess liquid has evaporated.

3. Combine potatoes with salt, pepper, thyme, rosemary, milk, bacon and onion/mushroom mixture.

A Lighter Side:

Omit bacon and cook onion and mushrooms in 1 tbsp/ 15 mL olive oil; use half the butter or use olive oil instead.

4. Work with one sheet of phyllo at a time, keeping the rest covered with a damp tea towel. Arrange one piece on baking sheet lined with parchment paper or foil. Brush with melted butter and sprinkle with breadcrumbs. Stack five more, adding melted butter and breadcrumbs to each layer.

5. Arrange half of filling down long end of phyllo. Roll up tightly to encase filling. Brush with butter. Repeat with remaining six sheets to make another strudel. Partially slice through the raw strudels at 3-inch/7.5 cm intervals to make slicing easier after they are cooked.

6. Bake in preheated 350°F/180°C oven for 1-1/2 hours, or until potatoes are very tender when pierced with knife. Cool for 10 minutes before slicing.

Harvest Spiced Strudel Pie

This pie looks and tastes spectacular. The filling can also be rolled into a more conventional strudel, as in the potato strudel (page 96), or it can be made into turnovers as in the Spanakopita (page 92, but make the triangles larger).

Makes 8 to 10 servings

FILLING:

5	apples (preferably Golden Delicious, Empire, Ida Red or Spy)	5
2	ripe pears (preferably Bartlett or Bosc)	2
1 cup	cranberries	250 mL
1/2 cup	brown sugar	125 mL
1/2 cup	chopped pecans, toasted (page 102)	125 mL
1 tsp	cinnamon	5 mL
pinch	nutmeg	pinch
pinch	allspice	pinch
1/4 cup	all-purpose flour	50 mL

PASTRY:

1/4 cup	dry breadcrumbs	50 mL
2 tbsp	granulated sugar	25 mL
14	sheets phyllo pastry	14
1/2 cup	butter, melted	125 mL
	Icing sugar	

A Lighter Side:
Use half the amount of butter. Omit nuts.

1. For filling, peel, core and slice apples and pears. Combine with cranberries, brown sugar, pecans, cinnamon, nutmeg, allspice and flour. Reserve.

2. To prepare pastry, have a 10- or 12-inch/25 or 30 cm springform pan at hand. Combine breadcrumbs with granulated sugar.

3. Working with one sheet of phyllo at a time (keep the remaining sheets covered with a damp tea towel), brush each sheet lightly with butter and dust with breadcrumb mixture. Fold pastry in half lengthwise and brush both sides lightly with butter.

4. Place pastry in pan with one end in centre of pan and the other end hanging over edge. Sprinkle with breadcrumb mixture. Repeat with remaining sheets, overlapping each slightly when you arrange them in the pan, and leaving a lot of pastry hanging over the edge. When you are finished, the bottom and sides of pan will be completely covered with overlapping layers of phyllo and the rest of strips will be hanging over the sides to fold up over the filling.

5. Spoon filling into pan. Fold pastry back over filling so it is completely encased (pastry will look somewhat ragged). Brush top of pie with any remaining butter. (If you want to build pie up even higher, fold and butter a few extra strips of phyllo pastry and sit them on top of the pie before baking.)

6. Bake in preheated 400°F/200°C oven for 15 minutes. Reduce heat to 350°F/180°C and bake for 40 to 45 minutes longer, or until pears and apples are thoroughly cooked when pie is pierced with sharp knife.

7. Cool for at least 15 minutes before removing pie from pan. Dust with icing sugar. Cut with a serrated knife.

12 Chocolate

TECHNIQUES AND TIPS

- *Good-quality European chocolate has a silkier and smoother texture than domestic chocolate; European semisweet or bittersweet is also less sweet and more chocolatey than most domestic versions.*

- *Unsweetened chocolate contains no sugar and has the strongest chocolate taste of any hard chocolate. Bittersweet has a strong chocolate flavour and the least amount of sugar, but it is still highly edible. Semisweet and sweet chocolate have more sugar and less chocolate taste. (Usually the sweeter the chocolate, the less chocolate taste it will have.) Milk chocolate contains sugar and milk, so it has even less chocolate flavour, and white chocolate does not contain the naturally strong-tasting chocolate liquor that colours and flavours dark chocolate so intensely, but it does contain the cocoa butter that gives chocolate its incredible texture.*

- *Chocolate burns easily and should never be melted on direct heat. To melt chocolate, chop it into small, even-sized pieces. Melt it in the top of a double boiler set over simmering water, or use Medium power in the microwave (follow the manufacturer's instructions). Allow the chocolate to melt to the point where the chopped bits look moist but have not completely lost their shape. Remove from heat and stir until the chocolate is completely melted.*

- *Plain unsweetened, bittersweet, semisweet and sweet chocolate will keep for 6 to 12 months, wrapped well, at room temperature. White chocolate or milk chocolate should be kept for 1 to 2 months.*

- *Chocolate may look streaky or white when stored for a while, but when it is melted, it will appear normal again.*

TECHNIQUE REVIEW

See this on the video

Hold the berry firmly and dip into melted chocolate.

Place the berry aside to dry. Then it can be double-dipped.

Brush crumbs off cake before glazing. Let a light glaze harden fully before final coat.

Spread the glaze and drizzle with white chocolate. Chocolate Celebration Cake (page 102) Chocolate-dipped Strawberries (page 104)

See this on the video

Chocolate Celebration Cake

This huge, wonderful cake is just the dessert to make special occasions really special. Serve it in small pieces, as it is rich and dense. If you don't have a springform pan, simply use a 13 x 9-inch/3.5 L baking dish that has been well-buttered and lined with parchment paper.

This cake can be served as is or with whipped cream and strawberries. As you can see from the video, for something really spectacular, add the chocolate glaze (page 105), drizzle it with melted white chocolate and surround the cake with chocolate-dipped strawberries (page 104). If you want to serve this for a smaller party, you can simply halve the recipe, and bake in an 8- or 9-inch/22 or 24 cm springform pan. The cake also freezes perfectly glazed or unglazed.

Makes a 12-inch/30 cm round cake (20 to 25 servings)

12 oz	bittersweet or semisweet chocolate	375 g
1-1/2 cups	butter	375 mL
8	eggs	8
1-1/2 cups	granulated sugar, divided	375 mL
2 cups	ground toasted pecans	500 mL
1/4 cup	all-purpose flour	50 mL
1/4 tsp	cream of tartar	1 mL

1. Butter 12-inch/30 cm springform pan and line bottom with a round of parchment paper. Butter lightly again.

2. Chop chocolate and cut butter into cubes. Melt together over gentle heat.

3. Separate eggs. Beat 1 cup/250 mL sugar with egg yolks until light.

4. Stir warm chocolate/butter mixture into egg yolks. Stir in pecans and flour.

Hint:

Toasting nuts increases their flavour. Place the nuts in a single layer on a baking sheet and bake in preheated 350°F/180°C oven for 3 to 10 minutes. Watch them closely to avoid burning.

5. Beat egg whites with cream of tartar until mounds begin to form. Slowly beat in remaining 1/2 cup/125 mL sugar. Beat until stiff but not dry.

6. Stir one-third of beaten egg whites into chocolate base to lighten it. Fold in remaining whites lightly. Spoon mixture gently into prepared pan.

7. Bake in preheated 350°F/180°C oven for 35 to 40 minutes, until toothpick inserted into centre comes out moist but not runny.

8. Cool cake in pan. Cake will be puffy and then fall, but don't worry. As the cake cools, press the sides down gently so that it is more even. Turn cake out onto a serving platter so that the flat bottom is now the top. (If you are decorating the cake with strawberries, use a large cake plate with room around the edge.)

9. If you are glazing the cake, make glaze. Cool slightly, but it should be runny when you use it. Brush off any crumbs from the cake, pour on a little glaze and spread it all over to seal in crumbs or "crumb coat" the cake. Pour remaining glaze over top of cake. Rotate cake slowly so that glaze coats top and sides and excess glaze runs onto the platter. (The excess glaze won't show when you put the strawberries around, and it actually helps to hold the strawberries in place.) Allow cake to set for a few hours before serving.

 See this on the video

Chocolate-dipped Strawberries

Chocolate-dipped strawberries are very easy to make, but there are a few tricks that will make them even easier:

- *The berries should be very dry when they are dipped into the melted chocolate. A drop of water can cause the chocolate to seize and become thick and dull-looking. (If that happens, warm the chocolate with a small spoonful of vegetable oil to smooth it out.)*
- *If the greens on the berries are nice, leave them on and dip the pointed end of the berry into the chocolate, using the stem as a handle. If the greens are wilted or dry, remove them and dip the wider end.*
- *Place dipped berries on a baking sheet lined with waxed paper or parchment paper. Refrigerate if necessary.*
- *Berries taste best when eaten on the same day they are dipped.*
- *Use the best-quality European bittersweet or semisweet chocolate for dipping berries. Do not add liqueur, butter or cream to chocolate that you are using to dip fruit, as this may cause the chocolate to seize or not harden properly.*
- *For an extra-special look, double-dip the berries — first into white chocolate and then, after they set, part way into dark chocolate.*

Makes about 32 berries

8 oz	bittersweet or semisweet chocolate	250 g
32	strawberries, washed and patted dry	32

1. Chop chocolate and place in bowl over simmering water or in the microwave in a 2 cup/500 mL glass measure or narrow, deep bowl (for easier dipping) on Medium power for 2 to 3 minutes. Stir to finish melting.

2. Dip strawberries part way into the chocolate and then place on waxed paper or parchment paper-lined baking sheets until set. Refrigerating the berries will speed up the setting, although the chocolate will probably lose its sheen.

All-purpose Chocolate Glaze

See this on the video

This glaze works beautifully on the Chocolate Celebration Cake (page 102), Chocolate Caramel Brownies (page 109) or any time you need a chocolate glaze that is firm but not brittle.

Makes about 1-1/2 cups/375 mL

12 oz	bittersweet or semisweet chocolate	375 g
3/4 cup	whipping cream	175 mL

1. Chop chocolate.

2. Combine chocolate with whipping cream. Heat gently until chocolate melts and mixes with the cream into a perfectly smooth glaze.

VARIATIONS:

For a chocolate mocha glaze, add 2 tbsp/25 mL instant espresso powder.

For a chocolate orange glaze, add 2 tbsp/25 mL orange liqueur.

For a chocolate raspberry glaze, add 2 tbsp/25 mL Chambord liqueur or Framboise eau-de-vie.

White and Dark Chocolate Cheesecake

A chocolate crust, a chocolate glaze and chocolate chips in the white chocolate filling make this a chocolate-lover's dream come true. It can be made a few days ahead and refrigerated, or it can be frozen for a few weeks. It is very rich, so serve it in small slices.

Makes 12 to 16 servings

CRUST:

2 cups	crushed chocolate wafer crumbs	500 mL
1/3 cup	butter, melted	75 mL

FILLING:

8 oz	white chocolate, chopped	250 g
1-1/2 lb	cream cheese	750 g
1 cup	granulated sugar	250 mL
3	eggs	3
1 tsp	vanilla	5 mL
1 cup	sour cream	250 mL
6 oz	bittersweet or semisweet chocolate, chopped, or 1 cup/250 mL chocolate chips	180 g

GLAZE:

4 oz	bittersweet or semisweet chocolate, chopped	125 g
1/4 cup	whipping cream	50 mL

1. Butter a 10-inch/25 cm springform pan.

2. Combine chocolate wafer crumbs and butter. Blend well. Pat into bottom of pan. Reserve.

3. Melt white chocolate in top of double boiler over gently simmering water or in the microwave on Medium for about 1 to 2 minutes. Remove from heat and cool slightly.

4. Beat cheese until very smooth and light. Gradually beat in sugar. Add melted white chocolate and eggs one at a time, beating well after each addition.

5. Add vanilla and sour cream and stir until blended thoroughly. Fold in 6 oz/180 g chopped dark chocolate.

6. Spoon mixture into pan. Bake in preheated 350°F/180°C oven for 50 to 55 minutes, or until cake is crusty on top but still slightly jiggly when gently shaken. Do not worry if cake cracks slightly, or seems slightly soft — it will firm up when chilled.

7. Remove cake from oven and run knife around inside edge of pan. Cool on rack and then refrigerate.

8. For glaze, melt 4 oz/125 g dark chocolate with cream and stir until smooth. Spread over top of cake and allow to set. Remove sides of pan. Serve on the pan base set on a cake plate. (It would be too difficult to remove cake from the base.) Refrigerate overnight. Serve cake very well chilled. Cut with a knife dipped in hot water.

Rocky Mountain Cookies

These "snow"-capped cookies require no baking. Use any dry cereal or cookies. They can also be made with milk chocolate.

Makes 38 cookies

1 lb	bittersweet or semisweet chocolate, chopped	500 g
2 cups	miniature marshmallows	500 mL
2 cups	crispy rice cereal	500 mL
1 cup	broken-up cookies	250 mL
1 cup	peanuts	250 mL
1/2 cup	dried cherries or raisins	125 mL
6 oz	white chocolate, chopped	180 g

1. Melt dark chocolate over gentle heat.

2. Combine marshmallows, cereal, cookies, peanuts and cherries.

3. Pour the melted chocolate over nut/cereal mixture and combine well.

4. Spoon mixture onto waxed paper-lined baking sheets in mounds that resemble (very roughly) little mountains.

5. Melt white chocolate. Spoon some white chocolate on each cookie and let it run down the "peak" like snow caps on a mountain.

Chocolate Caramel Brownies

Brownies taste spectacular with little bits of gooey caramel or candy bar throughout. These are rich enough as it is but, if you want to add a glaze, make half of the chocolate glaze recipe (page 105) and spread it on top. Allow to set in the refrigerator and then cut into squares. Brownies freeze well.

Makes 25 squares

5 oz	bittersweet or semisweet chocolate	150 g
1/2 cup	butter	125 mL
2	eggs	2
1 cup	granulated sugar	250 mL
1 tsp	vanilla	5 mL
1/2 cup	all-purpose flour	125 mL
1/2 tsp	baking powder	2 mL
pinch	salt	pinch
2	39 g Skor chocolate bars, chopped	2

1. Butter an 8- or 9-inch/2 or 2.5 L square baking pan. Line pan with parchment paper or waxed paper.

2. Melt chocolate with butter on gentle heat.

3. With a whisk, beat eggs with sugar and vanilla. Beat in chocolate mixture.

4. Stir flour with baking powder and salt.

5. Stir flour mixture into chocolate mixture. Stir in chopped chocolate bars.

6. Pour batter into prepared pan. Bake in preheated 350°F/180°C oven for 30 minutes. (Brownies may appear to be underbaked, but they will set when chilled.) Cool. Do not worry if sides are slightly higher than middle. Press sides down gently as brownies cool.

Index